GANDHIAN PHILOSOPHY AND HUMAN DEVELOPMENT

Gandhian Philosophy and Human Development

Edited by:

P.V. SARMA

KANISHKA PUBLISHERS, DISTRIBUTORS
NEW DELHI-110 002

KANISHKA PUBLISHERS, DISTRIBUTORS
4697/5-21 A, Ansari Road, Daryaganj
New Delhi-110 002
Phones : 2327 0497, 2328 8285
Fax : 011-2328 8285
E-mail: kanishka_publishing@yahoo.co.in

First Published 2008

ISBN 978-81-8457-020-5

PRINTED IN INDIA

Published by Madan Sachdeva for Kanishka Publishers, Distributors, 4697/5-21A, Ansari Road, Daryaganj, New Delhi-110 002, Typeset by Sunshine Graphics, Delhi, and Printed at Nice Printing Press, Delhi.

Preface

India is emulated and admired worldwide for the biggest victory of history, accomplished with the greatest weapons mankind has ever used i.e. Non-violence and truthfulness. However, in the recent times violence has become the order of the day and moral values have stooped down to an all time low. People are increasingly being influenced by the western culture and in the process moving away from our traditions, culture and value systems. At a time when the entire world is keen on practicing Gandhian principles, we are avoiding Gandhi. It is high time academicians, intellectuals and elders in the society should review seriously the situation and arrest this dangerous phenomenon by carefully nurturing the right values in the younger generation who are the future of the nation. This is very important at this juncture when the nation is poised to take off as a global economic leader because without the right social and ethical environment, no amount of economic development can contribute to improvement in overall quality of life.

Today, Gandhian philosophy is of more relevance and Gandhian values and principles for human development must be actively promoted among the present generation to help them lay the right foundation for a happy tomorrow. In this context Gayatri Vidya Parishad Degree College, Visakhapatnam has established a Center for the Study of Gandhian Philosophy and Human Development, to promote Gandhian principles among the younger generation in India. The Center organizes lectures, symposia, competitions etc., for students and staff to promote Gandhian thoughts. As part of such initiatives a National Seminar on Gandhian Philosophy and Human Development has been organized by the Center from February 16th-18th, 2007. The seminar focused on the following sub-themes:

- Gandhian Philosophy—Ethics and Values,

- Gandhi and Globalization,
- Gandhi and Women Empowerment,
- Gandhi and Sarvodaya Movement and
- Gandhi and Trusteeship.

A total of 25 chapters have been presented during the Seminar.

The proposed book is a collection of lectures delivered by eminent people from different walks of life who are striving to promote Gandhian views in the society, some of them in an abridged form. These chapters have been presented during various programmes organized by the Centre for the Study of Gandhian Philosophy and Human Development, Gayatri Vidya Parishad Degree College. It also has a few select papers presented in the National Seminar.

Sri S.N. Sahu compares Mahatam Gandhi to a management guru is he brings out the fact that Gandhi promoted all those principles of management which later on Peter Drucker became popular for. Mahatma Gandhi was a manager par excellence. His management was not based on any strategy or calculation but on deep conviction on certain fundamental principles and values which govern the whole universe.

Dr. P.N. Moorthy, focused on *The Mangerial Perspective of Gandhi's approach* to the struggle for freedom. Gandhi was a socially conscious management guru and hence he supported the dependency theory for effective management through team work. Managing to emancipate a single individual from poverty, which is the basis for economic freedom, was the ultimate task of Mahatma for which he propounded various methods of which truth, peace, non-violence turned out to be the cornerstones.

Sri G.V.V.S.D.S. Prasad, opines the social progress depends upon the attitudes of people that constitute it. He brings out the various forms of direct and indirect violence in the society. Corruption, Child Labour, Discrimination, Pollution etc., are all forms of violence which Gandhi had warned us about long ago. Values and ethics need to be revived to tackle this problem. People should check the greed within themselves and aspire for tolerance and brotherhood.

Dr. Madhu, Department of Psychology Andhra University and Director, Institute of Yoga and Consciousness, brings out the relevance of Gandhian ideas in the contemporary world. Gandhi's views on religious harmony, disarmament and peace, self-discipline, urbanization, environmental concerns, social order and global peace are accepted today worldwide and have been proved to be very much relevant.

Prof. C. Shambu Prasad, Xavier Institute of Management, Bhubaneswar, reminds everyone that Gandhi wanted his life to be a message. He expressed hope that Gandhism or Gandhigiri will help people to achieve their ambitions in life. However, very often it is being mistaken for Dadagiri and Buddhism. He suggests people should engage with Gandhi to understand him better.

Sri S.N. Sahu, Director, Prime Minister's Office, New Delhi, writes that the concept of non-violence followed by Gandhi was no ordinary idea or belief; it was born of a conviction and was based on the purification of the body and mind. It involved a complete change in the way of life and consciousness and remaining in communion with nature.

Sri K.S. Sastry focuses on the Gandhian approach to integrated rural development which he says is the most important issue in the context of globalization. Gandhi wanted village centered development. Sarvodaya is not against science and technology. He wants the latter to serve man rather than control him. Labour intensive technology should be adopted rather than aiming at mass production.

Sri P.A. Nazareth, formerly Ambassador of India to several countries and currently President—Sarvodaya International in his paper said that the promotion of Gandhian ideology to all Non-Gandhians is very important in the present scenario. Gita and Bible have inspired Gandhi to become a leader and he practiced the essence of the above two as a leader.

Dr. Anil Dutta Mishra, Deputy Director, National Gandhi Museum, New Delhi in his paper, raised the issue of human development which is a mark of true development of any nation and observed that the true wealth of any nation is its people only. He was critical about the ill effects of Globalization in the present context which results in concentration of economic power. While mentioning about the relevance of Gandhi to the above, he expressed the opinion that Gandhi has already mentioned in his book 'Hind Swaraj', in the year 1909, all the problems which the world is facing today. He stressed the need for experimenting Gandhian principles to derive the vision of Gandhi – "Gram Swaraj."

Prof. G. Ramachandrudu, Dr. G.A. Prabhakar and A. Rajani presented a chapter on "Gandhiji's Views and Globalization", in which they are of the opinion that, according to Gandhiji's theory of social reconstruction, practical application of the ideas of Ahimsa and Truth is the only logical way to stop the capitalistic way of exploitation of labour.

Dr. Madhukar and Mr. Surya Prakasa Rao, in their paper – "Economic of Ahimsa, Technology and Environment – Relevance of Gandhiji", concentrated on the modern way of organizing the important economic activities such as production, distribution and consumption comparing the concepts subjected to criticism, like over exploitation of resources for mass production by Gandhi, excessive importance to material growth and increasing standards of living by Sri J.C. Kumarappa, relative imbalances resulting between human and nature by Fritz Schemacher, a British Economist. The study highlights that application of non-violence (Ahimsa) never lead to conquer any human or economic activities.

Sri D.K. Oza, former Vice-Chancellor, Gandhigram University, Chennai, discussed the aspects relating to Corporate Social Responsibility (CSR) and suggested replacement of trusteeship with social audit. He says corporate sector must be invited and questioned on the issues related to their social responsibility. According to him, Gandhiji is larger than life, rather he is eternal. One should give utmost priority to inner freedom and strong belief to make a difference from others.

P.V.V.S. Raju and D.L. Deepak in their article – "Gandhiji's Alternative Economic Systems – Trusteeship" opined that Mahatma Gandhji opposed both capitalistic and bureaucratic views on ownership of properties. Analyzing the concept of Trusteeship, their study highlighted the need for management of properties by workers against the changes taking place in the present global era.

Sri Lavanam, freedom fighter and associate of Gandhi, shares his experiences in Sevagram in his paper and explains why Gandhi always wanted people to identify themselves with him. He is of the opinion that non-violence is the main source of Gandhi's concept of revolution. According to Sri Lavanam, every individual must always feel he/she is somebody and take pride in one's capabilities. Smt. P. Usha, in her chapter – 'Gandhian Thinking on Environment' focused on the problem caused by waste disposal, particularly solid waste and waste water disposal – in urban slums. She felt that a little effort on keeping our immediate surroundings clean can solve the problems of environment. She narrated, the damage being done to mankind by citing the empirical data given by the report on 14th U.N.World Water Day.

Dr. S.M. Murali Krishna and Mrs. P.V. Mohini presented their views on Gandhian relevance to Human Resources Development. While explaining the concepts such as Ahimsa, Dharma, Truth and Modernity they have opined that the Gandhian way of practicing Truth, Ethics and Non-Violence has more relevance in the existing global scenario. Their study, suggests that it is time to make a plan of action for implementing Gandhi's constructive programmes on a micro basis, especially Non-Governmental Organizations. Dr. G.A. Prabhakar and B. Siva Prasad, taking issues relating to Human Development and gender destinations presented a paper explaining the concept of Human Development.

I would like to thank all those who are associated with the Centre for the Study of Gandhian Philosophy and Human Development, especially all the eminent people from different parts of the country who are working to promote Gandhian values in the present society. I thank Prof. A. Prasanna Kumar for his advice and guidance in starting the Centre and organizing this Seminar. I thank all the participants of the Seminar and specially those who have contributed papers for the Seminar. I thank the Staff and students of GVP Degree College who have been participating very enthusiastically in the activities of the Centre. Above all I wish to thank the UGC for the financial support extended to this Center to organize various activities to promote Gandhian values.

P.V. SARMA

Contents

List of Contributors

Dr. S.M. Murali Krishna, Associate Professor, HOD, Gayatri Vidya Parishad, Degree and P.G. Courses, Visakhapatnam.

Mrs. P.V. Mohini, Assistant Professor, Gayatri Vidya Parishad Degree and P.G. Courses, Visakhapatnam.

A. Rajani, Faculty of Gayatri Degree College, Visakhapatnam.

C. Shambu Prasad, Associate Professor, Xavier Institute of Management, Bhubaneswar.

K.S. Sastry, Secretary, Gandhi Centre, Visakhapatnam, A Staunch Follower of Gandhian Ideology.

Dr. G.A. Prabhakar, Associate Professor, Department of H.R.M., G.V.P. Degree College, Visakhapatnam.

B. Siva Prasad, Assistant Professor, Department of H.R.M., G.V.P. Degree College, Visakhapatnam.

P.V.V.S.N. Raju, Assistant Professor, Department of H.R.M., G.V.P. Degree College, Visakhapatnam.

D.L. Deepak, Assistant Professor Department of H.R.M., G.V.P. Degree College, Visakhapatnam.

Alan Nazareth, Ambassador (Retd.), Managing Trustee, Sarvodaya International Trust.

G.V.V.S.D.S. Prasad, Secretary, A.P. Sarvodaya Mandal, Gandhi Bhavan, MJ Road, Hyderabad, A.P.

Dr. B. Madhukar, Associate Professor of Economics, G.V.P. Degree College,Visakhapatnam.

Mr. G. Surya Prakasa Rao, Assistant Professor of Economics, G.V.P. Degree, College, Visakhapatnam.

K. Visweswara Rao, Assistant Professor, School of Management Studies, G.V.P. Degree College, Visakhapatnam.

A.V. Jogarao, Assistant Professor, Department of H.R.M., G.V.P. Degree College, Visakhapatnam.

Mr. G. Surya Prakasa Rao, Assistant Professor of Economics, G.V.P. Degree College, Visakhapatnam.

Smt. P. Usha, M.A, M.Phil, Assistant Professor, Gayatri Degree College, Visakhapatnam.

Prof. G. Ramachandrudu, Professor, A.U., Visakhapatnam.

Sri S.N. Sahu, Director, Prime Minister's Office, New Delhi.

Dr. P.N. Moorthy, Director, Gandhian Study Centre, Pondicherry University, Pondicherry.

Dr. Anil Dutta Mishra, Deputy Director, National Gandhi Museum, New Delhi.

Sri. D.K. Oza, former Vice-Chancellor, Gandhigram University, Chennai.

Sri Lavanam, Freedom Fighter and Assoicate of Gandhi in Sevagram.

Prof. Madhu, Department of Psychology, Andhra University (A.P.).

1

Mahatma Gandhi as Management Guru

S.N. Sahu

Management is as old as human civilization. However, management as a discipline assumed importance after the Second World War and has emerged as one of the front ranking academic subjects in the world. The pursuit of management in prestigious institutions across the globe by bright and promising students testifies to its enormous relevance for our time. Professor Peter Drucker has been acclaimed as the founder of the management discipline and was being looked upon as a pivotal figure for making management one of the most sought after subjects in most of the countries. A perusal of Peter Drucker's writings reveals his philosophy behind the discipline of management and his postulates to make it a principal instrument to run modern organizations, enhance productivity and achieve success. The domain of management essentially encompasses in its scope the values and vision for efficiently running an enterprise and accomplish its stated goals.

After more than six decades of the introduction of management as a vibrant discipline one is pleasantly surprised to find that Mahatma Gandhi has been acknowledged as a Management Guru. The Harvard School of Business Management has hailed Mahatma Gandhi as Management Guru of the 20th century. Boston Consulting Group's CEO Arun Maira, prominent Professors of Management Professor C.K. Prahlad and Professor Arindam Chaudhury are now advocating to rediscover Mahatma Gandhi's ideas and leadership qualities for making managers more successful, humane and compassionate. Why is it that a discipline which emerged as a key discipline in western world is now looking up to Mahatma Gandhi for deriving inspiration to enrich its field, deepen its contributions and make it more worthwhile for addressing the contemporary challenges?

Mahatma Gandhi was a manager par excellence. His management was not based on any strategy or calculation but on deep conviction on certain fundamental principles and values which govern the whole universe. It is wrong to say that he was a strategist and therefore could succeed by following the well-crafted plans and formulations devised by applying the modern principles. His approach was as much based on spontaneity of action as on careful consideration of diverse issues confronting the nation, humanity and nature as a whole. His approach was far above the commonplace approach which stressed on outlays and outcomes and believed in a specific calculus to reach the goal. His management was born out of non-violence, care, compassion and modern values of liberty, equality and fraternity. Any attempt to manage the affairs of society and nation on the ideals of ancient civilization and contemporary human values will be of abiding significance for the modern managers.

It is indeed fascinating to note that the founder of the management discipline, Peter Drucker defined management in a manner which corresponded to the ideals of Mahatma Gandhi. It is a coincidence that Professor Drucker was born in 1909 when Mahatma Gandhi was in the midst of his first Satyagraha and wrote his first book 'Hind Swaraj' which criticized modern civilization based on multiplication of wants. When we refer to management the questions concerning spirituality or such other subtle aspects of life do not normally come to mind. However, the following observation of Peter Drucker is of immense importance to understand its deeper implications for human society and civilization. He wrote, "Because management deals with the motivation and direction of people in a common venture, it is deeply embedded in culture. A basic challenge Managers therefore face is to identify those elements of the traditions and culture of their workers that can be used as management building blocks. Besides, as everyone like myself, who have worked with Managers of all kinds of institutions for long years, have become aware, management is deeply involved with spiritual concerns—the nature of men, good and evil."

The spiritual concerns which form part of the above quotation is to my mind the most striking aspect of Peter Drucker's observation.

In Mahatma Gandhi's remarkable life and work we find spiritualism as the most determining force. Spiritualism here, of course, does not mean the conventional sense of going to a place of worship. It has a much more fundamental meaning of going beyond one's self and linking oneself with the larger society, the world and the universe. If we closely read Mahatma Gandhi's autobiography, we find that he was an extremely ordinary person with the frailties of a lesser mortal. Yet he was not overshadowed by the weaknesses of his personality and remained immersed in the negative attributes of his life. What he did was essentially the kind of a self-management to subordinate the negative impulses to positive qualities. As a young lawyer he went to South Africa and was subjected to racial discrimination and injustice. The negative treatment he received did not generate in him the same negative feeling to take revenge on the perpetrators of injustice. Rather in the Peters Martizburg Station, where he was thrown out of the first class compartment in spite of possessing of a valid ticket to travel, his active non-violence took birth. In other words, the positive learned traits prevailed over negative impulses to make him one of the shining examples of a Manager. And throughout his life he strove to ensure that the positive qualities reigned supreme over the negative attributes. A true manager is expected to cultivate such habits to "motivate and direct people for a common venture", to use the words of Peter Drucker. Gandhiji could do so by self-assessment and self-control. He was constantly evaluating his own actions and taking steps to control his anger and passion. This he started doing right from South Africa where he commenced his first Satyagraha which was launched not only to fight for the democratic rights of Indians but also to restructure the world on the basis of non-violence. He did so without the strength of money or political power. He had all the disadvantages in a foreign land. Yet by harnessing the sole force or the spiritual force he launched a mighty movement which succeeded to a large measure in getting back the rights to the Indians and above all heralding a new era of non-violent mass action for the larger goal of achieving justice and starting the process of reconciliation and understanding among different races of mankind.

In the above mentioned observation of Peter Drucker we noted his reference to spiritual concerns which a manager should relate itself while dealing with nature of human beings. 100 years back in South Africa Mahatma Gandhi studied the nature of human beings and adopted a spiritual path to address the problems arising out of suffering of his compatriots. If we read his book 'Satyagraha in South Africa' we learn that he was in quest of truth. He wrote that he saw truth in the suffering of the Indians. He then aimed to redress the sufferings to attain self-realisation and achieve truth. It is this larger goal of reaching out to truth by redressing the sufferings of the people made him one of the finest Managers in human history. The advent of such a Manager is a byproduct of a deeper spiritual conviction which took him beyond the material sphere and made him an outstanding Manager engaged in experiments with truth. He exercised self-control and subjected himself to self-assessment unremittingly and thereby took steps towards the final goal of truth which he said is the God. In his book 'Management–Tasks, responsibilities and practices' Peter Drucker devotes one small chapter on management and self-control. Much after Mahatma Gandhi subjected himself to self-control and spearheaded one of the epoch making movements for independence the founder of the modern management devoted his attention to self-control to prescribe methods to the modern managers for realizing the objectives of the organizations in which they worked.

It is well-known that Mahatma Gandhi accorded primacy to the means for achieving the ends. He stated that by employing noble means one could get equally noble results. This high minded ideal which he put into practice in his life is being now stressed by modern day managers. Peter Drucker whose name has been referred to earlier once wrote "Efficiency is doing things right and effectiveness is doing the right things." In other words, he suggested that just doing things right would not take us to a desired goal. Doing right things opens up possibilities for making our action more effective and more enduring. In the above statement of Peter Drucker one could realize the stress on right means for reaching the desired goal. We can apply appropriate means if we exercise restraint and cultivate values. It is being suggested by important managers in the modern organizations that the role of leadership must stress on making efficiency effective. And to make efficiency effective we need to do right things. One perspective admirer of Mahatma Gandhi and India from Austria, Mr. John Brussen wrote an interesting para for making our action more effective to run modern organizations. He used the famous equation of Einstein 'E = MC2'. It is well-known that one of the best comments on Mahatma Gandhi came from Einstein. He also described Gandhiji as the greatest political genius of the 20th century. Slightly altering the equation 'E = MC2' Mr. Brussen stated that if 'E' stood for excellence then 'M' stood for men and human beings and out of 'C2' one 'C' stood for commitment and the other for character. Thus, explaining the equation he stated that excellence could be achieved through commitment and character. This is exactly what Mahatma Gandhi did and this is exactly what the modern day managers are trying to emphasise.

Some of the distinguishing features of the modern day management practices revolve around total quality, customer relations, corporate social responsibility, human resource development, etc. If we closely examine the life and work of Mahatma Gandhi we find that he had taken up all these aspects while fighting for our independence. Let us take into account the total quality management which has become a defining feature of managerial practices since 1990s. Mahatma Gandhi stressed on quality in all his endeavours for mobilizing people for getting Swaraj. Quality here does not mean the quality of the product alone. Quality has to be reflected in every aspect of an organisation beginning from the process of production to the management of human relationship which are determining factors behind the production. Let us take the example of Gandhiji's conception of Swaraj. He was not merely concerned with the attainment of independence which, of course, remained one of the major goals of his non-violent struggle. He wanted to achieve quality Swaraj. But the quality Swaraj could not be achieved if Hindu-Muslim unity was compromised or untouchability persisted. He also linked the attainment of quality Swaraj to the quality of sanitation of our surroundings. He made a statement that if our backyards remained unclean then our Swaraj would have a foul stench. It is instructive also to note that he linked the quality Swaraj to the quality of our human resources. In other words, to reach the goal of quality Swaraj we have to achieve the quality Hindu-Muslim unity, the quality human relationships in terms of fraternity of all sections of society, empowerment of women, and above all the quality of our human resources. In today's management theory and practice, total quality means persistence of quality consciousness in every aspect of the organisation. That was what exactly Gandhiji did when he was in the forefront of the non-violent struggle for independence. To give an example of the total quality management of Mahatma Gandhi let us refer to this quotation relating to spinning. He wrote "Students must all do spinning in an scientific manner. Their tools will always be neat, clean and in good order and condition, then their yarn will naturally be of the highest quality." It is evident from the above observation of Gandhiji that to reach the final goal one has to ensure quality at every step. I pay my tribute to Mahatma for stressing on quality in every facet of life and spreading quality consciousness among people while engaging himself in the struggle for freedom.

We all know that customer care has remained at the centre of management practices. Peter Drucker once defined quality of a product from the point of view of customer. I think all of us are familiar with the remarkable observation of Mahatma Gandhi on customer. He wrote, "A customer is the most important visitor on our premises. He is not dependent on us. We are dependent on him. He is not an interruption in our work. He is the purpose of it. ...We are not doing him a favour by serving him. He is doing us a favour by giving us an opportunity to do so." The above observation on customer makes Mahatma Gandhi one of the foremost modern day managers whose thinking goes beyond the conventional understanding of management and covers the interests of customers and stakeholders who are the main purpose of business and commerce.

Again if we look at the idea of the stakeholder which is the governing principle of modern day business and management we find that Mahatma Gandhi had articulated such ideas much before the management authorities and experts had highlighted them. In one of the interesting books on Management written by Wayne Visser and Clem Sunter on the theme "Beyond Reasonable Greed : Why sustainable business is a much better idea?", it is stated that most of the modern day managers are driven by unreasonable greed and neglect the interests of the customers and shareholders. If we examine writings of Mahatma Gandhi from his collected works, we find that he gave importance to the workers and labourers in a factory as major stakeholders. His theory of Trusteeship essentially stressed on the responsibility of the owners of factories and wealth to treat their possessions as not entirely their own but as that of the society. On 31st March, 1936, he visited the Kollar Gold Mines and found that the small dwelling units of labourers lacked adequate space. He expressed deep regret that the mill owners were not giving adequate attention to the needs of the labourers. He then wrote "If the workers only knew what they could do for themselves by combining the training and intelligence they would realize that they were no less proprietors of the mines than the managers and the shareholders." By juxtaposing labourers with managers and shareholders, Gandhiji was emphasizing on a management method which if followed would ensure efficiency and effectiveness of an organisation. This is what exactly the modern day managers are doing while talking about maximizing the productivity of an organisation.

Earlier I had referred to the book "Beyond Reasonable Greed." In that book the authors have suggested that decline of ethics in many corporate organizations have resulted in financial irregularities and self-indulgence. He, therefore, suggested steps for reforming business. While doing do he also referred to Martin Luther of 1570 who attacked the then prevailing Church for self-indulgence and setting a wrong example before the people for leading a healthy life. His critical assessment of the mercenary practice of the Church and the opposition of the Church leaders for grandeur and wealth proved positive for the promotion of business. Mahatma Gandhi also exactly did the same thing by suggesting a restrained approach and self-control for better business practices. This approach of Gandhiji assumes relevance in the context of collapse of many corporations in the world on account of unethical practices. Now management students in many prominent management institutions are demanding introduction of courses on ethics.

In this context, let me refer to the kind of leadership which Gandhiji provided for the rest of the nation to follow. He identified himself with the common people and adopted voluntary poverty to tune himself to the ordinary masses. In fact in one of his letters to Hitler, before the beginning of the Second World War, he wrote "I can hear the dumb cry for peace from among the Europeans because I am tuned to the dumb millions of India." Mahatma Gandhi's exemplary leadership is a byproduct of his communion with the dumb millions of his country. Therefore, what the dumb millions did not have, he denied those things to himself. It was this exemplary leadership which need to be followed by the modern day managers for making their business practices more ethical and effective. On 24th February, 1942, Mahatma Gandhi wrote an interesting piece called "The duty of a Manager." He did so in response to a question which I am reproducing below:

> "Is it correct for the Head of an Institution, while demanding the utmost from his subordinates in the way of simple life, to live in comparative luxury himself even though the money he spends on himself be his own earnings."

The reply of Mahatma Gandhi to this question is not only fascinating but also educative. He wrote "The Manager who expects more from his co-workers than what he does is bound to fail." No wonder, therefore, that it is for his remarkable synchronization of words and action that Gandhiji became a model leader in the world. His example is now being followed by modern management institutes. Founder Director of Manford Alliance, Anand David wrote a special article on Mahatma Gandhi called the "Leader Mahatma" in the Training and Management journal in 2005. There he referred to Level-5 leaders who were humble and at the same time bold, modest and yet determined. They went beyond their personal gains and identified themselves with the larger cause of society, nation and humanity. Then Mr. Anand David wrote, "This is Gandhi to many of us." Such leadership qualities are used to motivate the personnel and optimize the competencies of the organisation. In the context of our struggle for our independence Mahatma Gandhi displayed that leadership quality which is now being emulated in rest of the world to fight for justice and equality and establish a more sustainable world order. The use of Mahatma Gandhi's picture in 1998 by the Apparel Computers in an advertisement testifies to the enduring relevance of Gandhiji for the modern day managers. In that advertisement there was just one picture of Gandhiji and below it, it was written, "Think different". So beyond the realm of politics Gandhiji assumes enormous significance in the corporate world.

Mahatma Gandhi stood for decentralization to devolve power and involve people in the process of governance. He did so when centralization was the governing norm. Through decentralization alone people can be given opportunities to play a meaningful role in running the affairs of the nation. It is very striking to note that in the field of management the idea of decentralization was accepted by managers in the 1960s. It was assumed that decentralization would lead to "top management abdication." Later it was realized that decentralization strengthens top management and makes it more effective. Adoption of the principles and practices of decentralization in the management domain is yet another example Gandhiji's relevance as a Management Guru.

Earlier a reference was made to the stakeholders. According to Mahatma Gandhi, "stakeholders are not only the people who possess the shares of a company but also all those who are linked to the activities of the organisation which has larger goal of serving society." Today when the emphasis is given on corporate social responsibility the idea of Mahatma Gandhi's theory of Trusteeship is of immense relevance for our time. In fact many business organizations are now stressing on a sustainable business practice which expand the scope of stakeholders to include the larger sphere of plants, animals and the whole environment. In the book "Beyond Reasonable Greed" which I had referred to earlier the authors have stressed on reforming business to go beyond the predatory commercial instinct and cultivate positive vision involving sustainable business in both a social and environmental sense. They have outlined the danger of following a lifestyle and using a product or business process which are unsustainable. It is very instructive to note that the authors used Mahatma Gandhi's famous words, "The Earth has enough for everyone's need but not for everyone's greed", and emphasized on a business practice which would look after the interests of not only human beings but also the nature. It is this larger understanding of the concept of stakeholder which remained central to such an approach. This is in consonance with what Mahatma Gandhi's advocacy of in 1930s for a doctrine of equality for all creatures. No revolution and movement which aimed at unchaining human beings from bondage had stressed on equality of all creatures. But now the modern day business people are talking about sustainable business practices so that they can continue their business activities in harmony with nature. This is what exactly Gandhiji meant when he wanted a doctrine of equality for all creatures. This idea must be incorporated in the larger scheme of management. No wonder, therefore, that Mahatma Gandhi has been described as the Management Guru of the 20th century.

2

Understanding Gandhian Concepts: Management Perspectives

Dr. P.N. Moorthy

Introduction

Mohandas Karamchand Gandhi was born on 2 October, 1869. After his school education in India, he went to England in 1888 to study law. In 1893, he went to South Africa as the legal advisor to an eminent merchant. During his stay in South Africa, he encountered many problems. However, the one faced by him in the train in 1893 at Pertermauritzburg in Johannesburg had great impact on his life and transformed him into 'Mahatma'. It is important to note such incident: "My name is Mohandas Karamchand Gandhi. I am a barrister. I have a first class ticket. Why should I go to the third class?" His opposition was ignored and he was kicked out of the train. Because of that incident, he launched a movement against racial discrimination practiced in South Africa, which helped remove the apartheid regime. He was also keen to consolidate the struggle by devising effective management technique – Satyagraha ('holding on to the truth') on September 11, 1906. After 21 years of his non-violent struggle in South Africa, he returned to India in 1914 and worked against British imperialism. For fighting against it, he founded the Non-Cooperative Movements in 1920, the Civil Disobedience Movement in 1930 and the Quit India Movement in 1942.[1]

As a great manager of his time and energy, he could advocate various thoughts in relation to managing the entire gamut of life starting from individual unit to global unit. Also, he was concerned, being a law professional, about moral values that are responsible for making law and practicing it. As a matter of fact, he could manage every affair of his life very effectively, of course, by using the teachings of Indian literature as he had no perpetual attraction towards western culture. Thus, he remained as a secular man with religious identity. However, his practice was based on scientific norms. He was ardent lover in seeking scientific truth – the foundation for any kind of research and he was always agreeable for amendment, for which he still remains in the hearts of the experts of management subjects as 'Management Guru' of the twenty-first century.

Gandhiji's attachment to the principles of scientific management can be understood from his following writings:[2] "I would like to say to the diligent reader of my writings and to others who are interested in them that I am not at all concerned with appearing to be consistent. In my search after truth I have discarded many ideas and learnt many new things. Old as I am in age I have no feeling that I have ceased to grow inwardly or that my growth will stop at the dissolution of the flesh. What I am concerned with is my readiness to obey the call of Truth, my God, from movement to moment, and, therefore, when anybody finds any inconsistency between any two writings of mine, if he has still faith in my sanity, he would do well to choose the later of the two on the same subject." Because of such scientific understanding, being a profound holistic thinker about the development of humanity, nature and their ecological interrelation – he was open in his learning process by introducing himself to various teachings such as Jains, Theosophists, Christians, Sermons, Ruskin, Shelly and Tolstoy and most significantly Bhagavad-Gita.

The Gandhian Basis of Management

As stated above, Mahatma Gandhi could manage every affair of his life efficiently. In most of his life, he was identified with the poorest of the poor. He worked for their enlightenment both in India and in South Africa. His fight for social emancipation was greatly appreciated by the world leaders. He believed, therefore, in the management mantra: 'management is making ordinary people produce extraordinary result not getting things done by people.' Accordingly, he fought against social enslavement with the conviction that poor people should be freed from slavery not only in the physical sense but also in their mental states. In his writings, he noted with concern: "There is no freedom for India (or the world as a whole) so long as one man, no matter how highly placed he may be, holds in the hollow of his hand the life, property and honour of millions of human beings... It is an artificial, unnatural and uncivilized process."[3] Therefore, he recommended self-freedom, Swaraj. For him, Swaraj is the catchword not only for national freedom but also managing economic, social and psychological problems. The importance attached to the establishment of Swaraj may be noted from the following quotation of Mahatma Gandhi: "Recall the face of the poorest and the most helpless man whom you have seen and ask yourself, if the step you contemplate is going to be of any use to him. Will he be able to gain any by it? Will it restore him to a control over his own life and destiny? In other worlds, will it lead to Swaraj or self rule for the hungry and also spiritually starved millions of your country men? Then you will find your doubts and your self melting away."[4] He also noted with concern for taking the responsibility in promoting the welfare of the fellowmen. In this process social emancipation should be achieved for the successful management of the Swaraj not only at the individual level but also at the global level.

Managing to emancipate a single individual from poverty, which is the basis for economic freedom, was the ultimate task of Mahatma for which he had time and again propounded various methods of which truth, peace, non-violence turned out to be the cornerstones. Being a socially conscious management guru, he supported the dependency theory for effective management of a set goal through team works. In this fashion, he had established Ashrams in various parts of the world to render unique training to the inmates of Ashram. According to him, all should work physically to enjoy their food. Also, he was particular that everyone should work for fulfilling the need not the greed. In fact, he made every individual, including his wife and children, participate in the team work in the Ashram.[5] In the political front too, Ganhdiji advocated simple principle for managing political crisis. According to him, political freedom is something, which is needed for every individual. As he notes, an individual development has to be the ultimate object of political exploration as the star is the ultimate body of astronomical exploration. The entire exercise, therefore, should be around an individual, man or woman, leading to benefits not destructions. It is interesting to have this comparison, as the star is believed to be the 'life giver' for the entire earth, and the man is the 'life giver' for the entire gamut of politics. Therefore, Gandhiji advocated his political philosophy by taking man as a centre of all activities. According to him, theory and practice in politics should be equal and should be followed in a balancing way aiming at uplifting an individual economically. As view by Gandhi that if a person is self-punishing for his/her own mistakes himself/herself, the politics he/she does would help the human kind, if not, even if the philosophy is good, will not work in practice.[6]

Gandhiji, therefore, advocated a holistic framework for his ideals with a profound concern for individuals. According to it, a man should be 'environmental friendly'. If he is not, the environment will create many problems. This is where we are all landed in the present world. In this connection, it is important to note Toynbee who noted that 'if we don't abolish war, war will abolish us'. Similarly if the industrialization/unwanted competitive business of any kinds are not checked up, it is going to spoil the entire life setting very badly which will therefore lead us towards destructions. It is better to note here the Gandhian quotation on industrialization: "my own view is that evils are inherent in industrialization and no amount of socialism can eradicate them."[7] Thus, Gandhiji was clear in his advocacy that the mechanical/machine/industrial/artificial life would create problems, which would lead the humankind to the point of no return. It should be noted that Gandhiji never hated industrial development, but the inhuman face of industrial planning which causes the replacement of human with machine. Thus, he advocated for a non-violence oriented industrial economy realizing the management mantra that the productivity of men's capacity is more important than industrial/plant capacity. It is amply clear that love erected on the basis of peace and non-violence is the central one in the management techniques of Mahatma Gandhi for the cause of promoting the humanity.[8]

World Leaders' Perception

It is important to note some of the views of prominent persons on Mahatma Gandhi. "Gandhi's Truth"—a book written by Eric Erickson compares Gandhiji's personality with the personality of Jesus Christ. The writings of the great French writer and well-known Peace-maker of his time, Romaine Rolland compares Gandhiji with St. Paul of our age—a Jew turned out to be Christian and who had become martyr in 64 or 67 A.D., as he was ordered to be killed by the Government. Albert Einstein said once: "It is my belief that the problem of bringing peace to the world on a supranational basis will be solved only by employing Gandhian's methods on a large scale." He had also stated further describing Gandhiji as "a light-house to the future generations."[9] Martin Luther King said: "From my background, I gained my self by regulating Christian ideals. From Gandhi, I learned my operational technique."[10] Rev. Dr. John Haynes Holmes, Minister of the Community Church of New York had said: "Already Gandhi's place in history is sure. Our age is blessed by the presence of one more of the pure leaders of the spirit. Amidst the fury of force and violence, bloodshed and slaughter, these save mankind from death, and patiently and ever steadfastly point the way to life."[11] Louis Fisher, American Correspondent and Commentator, wrote; "I have met Lenin, Churchill, Franklin D. Roosevelt, Wilkie, Stalin, Lituvinov, Attlee, Einstein, Lloyd George, Eleanor Roosevelt and many other famous people. I have never met a more remarkable person than Gandhi."[12]

The strategists of nuclear weapons, Henry Kissinger notes in his writings that "Gandhiji's life was inspired by truth, which had no boundary in space and time and which could only be the base for the edifice of peace and non-violence in the world."[13] Similarly Kenneth Boulding notes, "The road to life, to government and to organization always leads uphill. The easy roads, the intrinsic dynamics, always lead downhill to ultimate destruction...where then are new ideas and new images of the future that look like upward paths? One is clearly the idea of the non-violent resistance associated with the name of Gandhi... This is a powerful method of bargaining for a social contract."[14] In a lucid and honest way, Boulding approves of Gandhian ideas on non-violence as a new way of life for managing not only individual problems but also the problems of the world community. The former President of South Africa and the ardent follower of Mahatma Gandhi, Nelson Mandela in 1999 aptly pointed out that the twenty-first century would be the Gandhian century.[15]

In this line of thinking, the world leaders at United Nations had declared this first decade of the twenty-first century (2000-10) as the 'International Decade of Culture of Peace and Non-Violence' to explore the possibilities for implementing Gandian techniques for managing the problems of the world ranging from politics to economics. Twenty Nobel Laureates have pledged their commitment to this cause and have emphasized the need to spread the message of non-violence at every level of society during this decade. 189 countries have adopted this historic 'Millennium Declaration' in their national agenda and have been working for achieving peace, prosperity and human development in the twenty-first century through the set agenda of the UN Eradicate extreme poverty and hunger; Achieve universal primary education; Promote gender equality and empower women; Reduce child mortality; Improve maternal health; Combat HIV/AIDS, tuberculosis, malaria and other diseases; Ensure environmental sustainability Promote peace and human right. It should be noted here that most of the schemes of the UN are from Constructive Programeme of Mahatma Gandhi devised during 1920-47.[16] Thus, Ganhian ideals have become much more important than ever before for managing the problems of world community.

Essentials of Gandhian Management

Peace and non-violence are the mantras of Mahatma Gandhi derived from his careful readings on four Purshartha of human life: Dharma – good values: Artha – economic pursuit of wealth, power etc; Karma – desire fulfillment and pursuit of pleasure; Moksha – emancipation from the ego and discovery of one's true nature as atman or soul.[17] Thus, he constructed a bridge of relation with scientific Hindu tradition, keeping himself away from the unscientific religious practices, for taking the advantages from the Indian Management Ethics (IME) based on its own cultural ethos. It should be realized here by all the students of management science that every nation has got its own management identity based on its own cultural ethos. For instance, the British make loyalty as management mantra, the American – performance, the Japanese – based on Buddhism and Confucianism and the European based on Protestant beliefs. Similarly, India's management mantra is based on 'empowerment of man', the concept realized by the leading experts of management studies like Abraham Maslow, Herzberg and Peter Drucker in the later stage. The Indian ethos of management is based on the following basic principles:[18] Unleashing Infinite Potential (*Tat Tvam Asi*), Holistic Approach (*Atmano Mokshya Jagat Hitaaya ca*) and Subjectivity (*Sukshma*). The core of the element in the dynamics of all the above discourse of Indian ethos of management is as follows:[19] "Each soul is essentially divine. Discovering divinity is the purpose of work."

Ganhiji had considered the core element of IEM and accordingly developed his philosophy for the 'empowerment of people' based on the culture of India and advocated for peace and non-violence. To him, peace and non-violence are by-products of love, the centre of non-violent knowledge. Non-violent knowledge is the one that contributes for peace, prosperity and human development without any discrimination. Hence, a product of science and technology is nothing but a product of love. Because of the dedication of a person who spends time and energy devoted with love of involvement in the process of production, the humanity benefits using it. Without love of knowledge that has no boundary or prejudice, human prosperity is impossible. The following sections attempts to understand the dynamics of the essential elements of Gandhian philosophy.

Truth

Gandhian concepts are the results of self-exploration. A self testified philosophy should only, according to him, be advocated to anyone. If not, as he pointes out it will never work. For applying a concept in a practical setting of life one should be truthful which is what Gandhiji more often stressed upon. Truth, being the God to him, he wanted everyone adopt truth as a central one in their cycle of life. He notes:[20] "It should be an essential of real education that a child should learn that, in the struggle of life, it can easily conquer hate by love, untruth by truth, violence by self-suffering." Such dynamics of love may be understood in the following way.

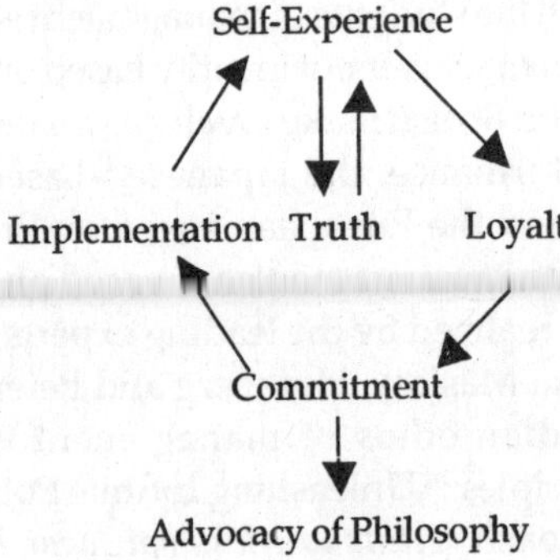

Peace

A truthful person will be gifted with peace of mind. A peace of mind therefore leads him environment friendly with fellow human beings as well as nature. Therefore, as Gandhiji stressed, "Peace is the temple or church of truth."[21] Once that is being achieved in human beings he or she will be a productive peace-maker. A non-productive person has no right, according to Gandhiji, to enjoy the fruits from the sources of nature. He or she has to therefore labour that too through peaceful means. This type of peace dynamism can be, understood from the following diagram:

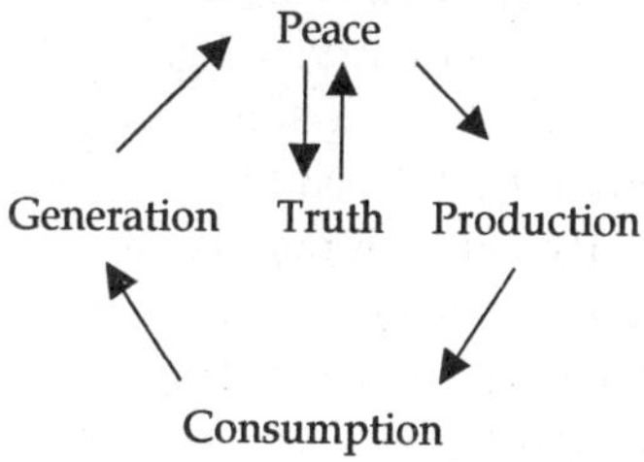

Non-Violence

If the truth and peace were with an entity of human kind, there would be cycle of non-violence creating more rings all over. Gandhi states: "Non-violence is not a garment to be put on an off at will. It is in the heart, and it must be an inseparable part of our very being."[22] As Gandhiji says non-violence is part of every individual. He or she should carefully utilize it for the cause of empowering not only him or her but also the entire humanity. Such work will bring fruits only when all are free of hunger, discrimination, exclusion, intolerance and hatred. If we don't attain such state, violence will crop up certainly in the society. If the non-violent methods of Mahatma are implemented for managing any problems starting from any individual unit level to collective level for the purpose of collective survival or peaceful co-existence, there will be cycle of non-violent functions widening the path for attainment of violence free knowledge society. Such dynamics is explained below:

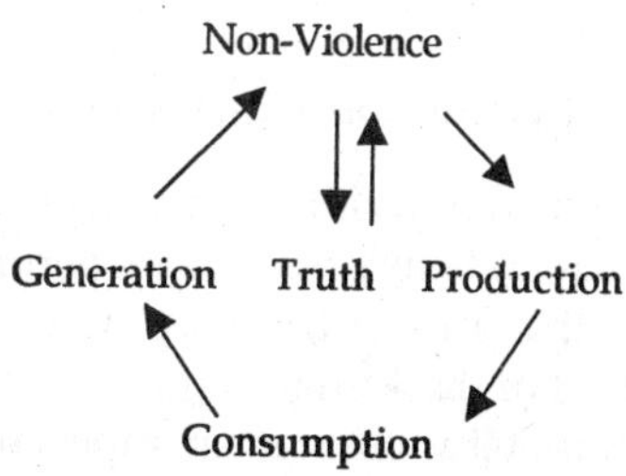

Love

For being truthful, peaceful and non-violent, one should learn the "black hole of love." It is black hole-like-dynamic concept because if one loves to suffer or to enjoy in a same way with same feeling it can be stated that one achieves to be a love centered man.[23] Placing one in that love centered order is attached with self-emancipation through self-suffering. According to Gandhiji, love is the element of truth. In other words, love is the one ray of light in the universe of truth. Without love therefore it is impossible to be a truth-oriented person. For perfect exposition of understanding in this respect, it is better to note Gandhiji's quotation. It reads: "Truth in action is ahimsa, love. Truth and love, satya and ahimsa, are like the two sides of a coin. All great religions enjoin the practice of love...non-violence is complete innocence. Complete non-violence is complete absence of ill will against all that lives. Non-violence is innocence in its action form, good will towards all life. It is pure love... Hatred deflects our thinking; endanger the very sense of humanity. Love of power takes the place of conscience."[24] This self-explanatory analysis of Gandhiji on the dynamics of love can be explained in the following way:

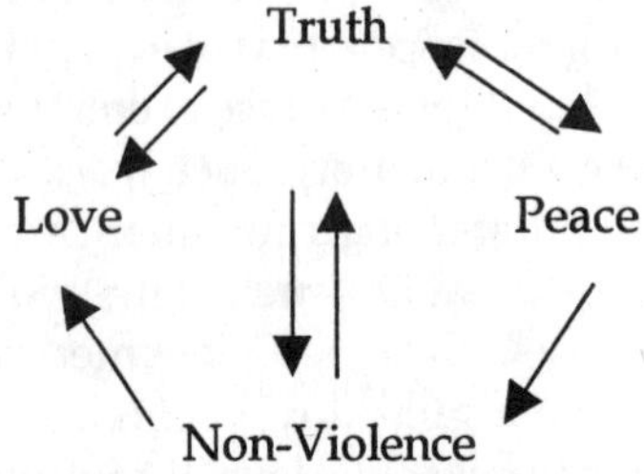

These four dynamic concepts of Gandhiji, if truly adopted, would work as nuclei of atom, which would help achieve "thermo nuclear peace" at a larger scale, which is needed for the present world.

Widening the Net of Gandhian Management

Once it is achieved in an individual unit level, there cannot be any problem to implement it to any other level of other units leading to the entire globe. In this process there would be advantages as well as disadvantages. For tackling them in a regulated scale of implementation, Gandhiji advocated an important technique known as "Satyagraha, which was identified by him with truth-force, soul-force, tapasya, dharmayudh."[25] It is nothing but insistence on truth. Truth has to be, as he stressed, followed carefully with the realization of two important concepts such as self-punishment and passive resistance. Gandhian concept of 'self-punishment' is a humble one, which is soul searching in a simplistic explanation. As a satyagrahi knows that a force would bring only force one has to undergo sufferings so as to make others realize his or her self-suffering situation in order to achieve the objective of convincing those joins him or her Satyagraha movements.[26] If the self-suffering practice doesn't work and the other side is so adamant in realizing the truth of the satyagrahi according to Gandhiji, can go for 'passive resistance' practice such as non-violent strike or demonstration, generating public opinion, fast and non-cooperation. Thus, the dynamics of his or her action through Satyagraha would lead for exploring into a real non-violent peace. This is shown in the following diagram:

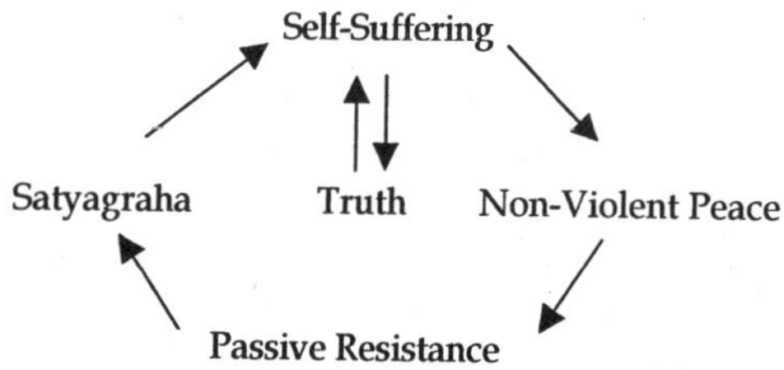

Thus, Satyagraha, therefore, becomes a "cell of action" without which peace in a real sense and in a greater scale can never be achieved. Satyagraha, as Gandhiji noted, is not an idealistic concept but it is practical and dynamic one. According to him, it has to be implemented in order to achieve the objective of peace in a given condition. He considered this as the only means for obtaining peace. For him, therefore, Satyagraha was everything. As he notes, it can achieve not only local peace but also the international one. Therefore, an internationalist interested in this effort should hold firmly the truth and bravely wage the war of peace against unjust and violent world order. This type of international Satyagraha should be, as guide lined by Gandhiji, on the basis of non-violent world order of action that includes non-violent mass action. To become a perfect non-violent soldier in this struggle Gandhiji put forward the following pre-conditions for individuals:[27]

- *Non-violent attitude towards nature:* It is necessary for any peace-loving person to be aware of his or her environment.
- *Love towards all creation:* This outlook is an essential part of an individual spirituality.
- *Love towards fellow creatures:* According to Gandhiji, all creatures are God's children and therefore the peace-makers of the world should love them all.
- *Love at the risk of their life:* A satyagrahi should possess this quality, which will make him very consolidate in his effort for achieving international peace.
- *Love towards the cosmos:* It helps the individuals to be universal in their outlook.
- *Non-resistance to aggression:* It makes them to be absolute in their non-violent action.
- *Amity through non-violence:* It teaches the individuals the power of living together.
- *One man boundary force:* According to Gandhiji, peacemakers should not fear to be alone in their fight.
- *Martyr for the principles:* Through his non-violent practice, Gandhiji developed a wonderful idea for the permanent peace of the world. He developed a new concept, 'Shanti Sena', which means 'Peace Brigade'. It was a powerful and indeed revolutionary concept of his time. Every individual should, therefore, join the peace brigade by resenting him or her as a soldier of peace.
- *Martyrdom:* According to Gandhiji, a true peace soldier should even lay down his or her life for the cause of peace and communal harmony in the process of peace struggle.

Gandhian advocacies for better management, therefore, rest in the following recommendations. He notes that one has to avoid the seven social evil: politics without principles, wealth without work, pleasure without conscience, knowledge without character, commerce without morality, science without humanity, and worship without sacrifice. For practice, he puts forward another eleven Vratas for everyone to observe: Truth (for him it is *ananda*), *ahmsa*, *brahmacharya* (chastity, i.e., truth finder not by any ordinary meaning), aswad (control of the palate-eating habit related), *asteya* (non-stealing), *Aparigrah* (non-possession), *abhaya* (fearlessness), *asprishyata-Niwaran* (removal of untouchability), *sharir-shram* (bread lobour), *sarva dharma samabhav* (tolerance and equality of all religions), *swadeshi* (service of the immediate neighbours). For helping out the society, he recommends the following constructive programme: communual unity, removal of untouchability, prohibition, khadi, other village industries, village sanitation, basic education, adult education, women welfare, education in health and hygiene, provincial languages, economic equality, adivasis. [28] As he noted that 'if you want change be a change your self', change in attitude is necessary pre-condition to become a better managers of the present world who should give more importance to both holistic doing. Therefore, globalizing Gandhian ideals have become much more important in this 'crisis prone world' for every management conscious individuals. In fact, as noted above, the entire world expects much from the ideals of Mahatma. As Swamy Chinmayananda notes in his book: 'Awakening Indians to India', Indians should guide the world responsibly realizing the ideals of Mahatma.[29]

Conclusion

Effective management cannot be achieved without realizing the concepts and techniques of Gandhiji. The present order for achieving human prosperity which is the central theme of management, as described above, rests on violence, force and power or unwanted completion among people, which create a cycle of violence among nations. It leads, as experienced, to unhealthy competition and therefore violence all over the world. This can be explained as follows.

Use of Force
(Business based on maximization of profit by any means)
↑↓
Violence
↑↓
Tensions
↑↓
Armaments
(Spiral of unethical business)

Gandhiji on the other hand suggests that 'love' could be adopted as the 'means ' for achieving non-violent or 'perfect peace'. To him peace without love is violence and love without peace is also violence. Therefore, the concept love should work replacing the use of force all over. It is explained in the following diagram:

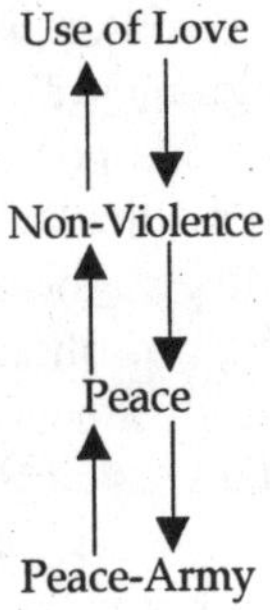

According to Gandhiji, the ultimate goal of any peace-maker should be of building-up of peace army. It is necessary to quote here the Gandhiji's statement. It reads..."the moral principles on which civilization rest are truth and love. If people everywhere respond to them truthfully, the world will be brought closer together and the darkness of violence which we see around us may be dispelled." [30] For he codifies eleven owes to be adapted as follows as management mantras: Satyagraha, Ahimsa, honesty, simple living, physical labour, swadeshi, fearlessness, control of the tongue, brahmacharya, equality of classes and equality of religions. On the basis his proposition if the management experts of the world community work in unison with the support of the UN, the twenty first century will be the century of peace, prosperity and human development.

REFERENCES

1. See Eric Erickson, *Gandhi's Truth: On the Origins of Militant Non-violence* (New Delhi: Norton and Company, 1989), pp. 66-96.
2. Cited in N. Radhakrishnan (edi), *Gandhian Perspective of Nations Building for World Peace* (New Delhi: Konark Publishers, 1992), p. 142.
3. See M.K. Gandhi, *Hindu Swaraj or Home Rule* (Ahmedabad: Navajivan, 1990), pp. 18-20.
4. Cited from S. Kulandhaisamy, *A True Friend* (Chennai: Gandhi Peace Foundation, 2006), p. 7.
5. See for more details on Truth, M.K. Gandhi, and Ruskin *Unto this Last* (Ahmedabad: Navajivan Press, 1998), pp. 3-17.
6. *Ibid;* See the *Collected Works of Mahatma Gandhi* (Ahmedabad: Navajivan Press, 1958.

7. Cited in S.N. Prasad and Suman Shukla (edit.), *Gandhi, Non-Violence and Peace* (Ambala Cantt: Associate Publishers, 1995), p. 22.
8. *Ibid.*
9. Cited from S. Kulandhaisamy, *The Mahatma In Us* (Chennai: Gandhi Peace Foundation, 2006), pp. 84-85.
10. *Ibid.*
11. *Ibid.*
12. *Ibid.*
13. See Edward Haley, David Keithy and Jack Merritt (edit.), *Nuclear Strategy, Arms Control and the Future* (London: Westview Press, 1985), pp. 37-54 .
14. *Ibid.*
15. See *The Hindu* (Madras), 22 March, 1999.
16. *United Nations New Bulletin* (New Delhi), 22 December, 2000; also for future Perspectives on Gandhian economic plan see Gunvant Shah, *Gandhi for the New Generation* (Ahmedabad: Navajivan Press, 1982).
17. See Swamy Chinmayananda, *Awakening Indians to India* (Mumbai: Chinmaya Mission Trust, 2003), pp. 211-15.
18. *Ibid.*
19. *Ibid.*
20. Cited from S. Kulandhaisamy, *New World* (Chennai: Gandhi Peace Foundation, 2006), p. 32.
21. See for more details on Truth, M.K. Gandhi, and Ruskin *Unto this Last* No. 5, pp. 3-17.
22. *Ibid.*
23. *Ibid.*
24. *Ibid.*
25. See S.N. Prasad and Suman Shukla (edit.), *Gandhi, Non-Violence and Peace*, No. 7, p. 22.
26. *Ibid.*
27. For more detail see See the *Collected Works of Mahatma Gandhi* (Ahmedabad: Navajivan Press, 1958).
28. See, N. Radhkrishnan, *Gandhi Youth and Non-Violence: Experiments in Conflict Resolution* (Mithrapuram: Centre for Development and Peace, 1992), pp. 12-16.
29. See for perspectives in this regard, Swamy Chinmayananda, *Awakening Indians to India*, No. 17.
30. M.K. Gandhi and Ruskin *Unto this Last* No. 5, p. 16.

3

Gandhian Philosophy and Its Relevance to Human Resources Development

Dr. S.M. Murali Krishna and Mrs. P.V. Mohini

Gandhi is a pre-eminent theorist of non-violent disobedience, the leader of Indian's successful campaign for national independence and an architect of modern Indian self-identity.[1] He offers a powerful deference of autonomy and a critique of modernity and modernization. He seeks a peaceful world, a stable society and a coherent spiritual life.

Gandhi advocated Ahimsa, Non-Violence, Dharma and truth. Autonomy stands at the centre of Gandhian political philosophy. People deserve the freedom to pursue their moral project honesty and they have the duty to do so. Each person should be free from both domination and violence. Addressing the needs of the most vulnerable members of society is an essential requirement. No one is given leave to force others to do. All individuals are fundamentally equal; diversity is respected and the quest for domination is replaced by cooperation. The people are expected to be active participants concerned not only with their own—self-governance but also to the autonomy of each other. The prominence of autonomy was seen in his programme for swaraj or self rule—for India. He says that complete Indian independence means the conversance in the average villager that he is the made of his own destiny. The Indian's must learn to rule themselves, individually and collectively.[2] Theories of autonomy assume that people are ultimately responsible for the moral character that grows out of their choice. Freedom is necessary for autonomy, but Gandhi says that freedom is not necessary at theoretical level but essential at practical level. People have both a moral or biological nature and the latter has a more completing nature. To make mistakes as a free man is better than being is bondage in order to avoid them. The mind of a man who remains good under compulsion cannot improve, infact, it worsens.[3]

Ahimsa

Ahimsa means not injuring any living being, whether by body or mind or bear any ill to him and so cause him mental suffering. It is a negative approach. But, positively, it means an unbounded love for all.[4] Himsa means doing injury to others. He further defines, Ahimsa as hunting by every evil thought, by undue haste, by lying, by hared or wishing ill of anybody. Ahimsa is more than avoiding harm. It is the largest love, the greatest charity. He says "if I am a follower ahimsa, I must love my enemy."

Himsa is inherent necessity for life in the body. We must make ... endeavour to reduce the circle of Himsa.

In our ancient culture too Himsa is detested. Non-violence (Ahimsa) is the foremost of the Yamas. Ahimsa implies not to harm others whether by thought, word or deed. It is considered as a virtue to be practiced for & fostering universal brotherhood in human societies and nations all over the world.[5]

Gandhi says, "it is impossible to avoid harming others not because we are evil but because human life rotates around both our spiritual and biological nature." No activity is possible without a contain amount of violence. What we have to do is to minimize it to the greatest extent possible indeed the very word, non-violence.

Dharma

Gandhi often resorts to Dharma to express his views to the duties of the community, to remind us how to act and what we owe others. In his views of cosmology everyone has an individual Dharma covering multiple duties and needs. Dharma is the foundation of the whole universe.[6] Dharma was advocated in ancient scriptures as it drives away the evil. It is called the highest good in Taitterya Aranyaka. Dharma is resorted for the sake of promotion of strength and efficiency among beings. Whatever, is attended with the non-violence, that is Dharma. Dharma pressures when preserved, destroys when violated.

Gandhi's concept of Dharma is related to his views on moral projects. He insists that Dharma is not satisfied only by performing the duties that are attached to the specific role of a person but should serve the society as well.

In ancient India, the scriptures have encouraged individuals to strive for *Dharma* – (Social order and discharge of obligations), *Artha* (generation, conservation and distribution of wealth and knowledge) *Kama* (sensory pleasure, art and literature) and *Moksha* (spiritual liberation total satisfaction from life) through purushardha (activism).[8]

Gandhi emphasized the need for following Dharma in modern age which implies one's duties and obligation towards others through rightful thoughts, means and actions. He believes that modern emphasis is on economic production and consumption which narrows the projects of individuals who are for earning increasingly insular and materialistic. So, he feels that a way act of this confusion is to rely on tradition.

Tradition forms the foundation for choice and action – yet; it is not exempt from normal serutiny. Gandhi did not entirely rely on tradition saying that something ancient does not mean that it is beyond criticism, and necessarily worth while.[9]

He declares, "I cannot let a scriptural text suppress act my reasons."

He condemns the traditions that are contrary to universal truths and morals, or in conflict with reasons. He advises one's reasoning in accepting a tradition. The validity of a tradition is to be tested on the touchstone of autonomy. Tradition is sound when it celebrates the dignity of all persons and provide good material for the good of one's life and of the community.

He defends to nourish local traditions where individuals live and work which provide them with purpose and dignity. He confronts modern version of fatalism.

Truth

When Gandhi declares that truth is God, he means that truth transcends our biological natures and rises above the forces of gravity. Though the truth as expressed by individuals from their religions and moral commitments differ; they essentially share the same moral core in respecting dignity of persons. Devotion to truth is the sole reasons for our existence. He wants is to be fully humane, and honest to what we take to be true. They must be honest to themselves (our selves), even if it leads to our own suffering.[10]

Different traditions include fragment of truth but its totality remains elusive to anyone person or tradition. Respecting different approaches to the truth is itself an embodiment of truth.[11]

Comprehensive truth exceeds the human capacities to know and control. Gandhi's truth always speakes to autonomy, equality, and dignity of person and resists domination and humiliation. Real truth is found in life itself. God cannot be found apart from humanity.[12]

In our ancient culture too truth was mentioned as one of the five Yamas, the other being non-violence (*Ahimsa*) non-misappropriation (*Asteya*), celibacy (*Brahmacharya*) and detachment (*Aparigraha*).[8] The vedic seriptures clarifies that truth (*satya*) is the persuit of factual knowledge and consonance in thoughts, words and deeds.

Modernity

Some hold the view that we cannot escape complexity, cannot avoid centralization, cannot resist globalization of modern culture and that we cannot repeal the inevitability of violent conflict or the growing impersonality of a world that judge the good in terms of its economic contribution.

Through it is impossible to return to earlier cosmos, he wants to apply continually ethical standards to contemporary practices and institutions. He rejects the modern tendency to make economic criteria the standard for judging persons and institutions. He says, it degrades the humanity. Accelerating for greater centralization, coordination and hierarchy encroach on autonomy. He emphasizes that people ought to govern themselves. Power has to be dispersed and participation thought the society has to be encouraged.

Gandhi warns about globalization of modern economy not only because of its economic effects but also because it is accompanied with the globalization of culture. He asserts that local cultures are critical because, each of the culture provides a concrete sense of identity and meaning apart from productivity and consumption. Tradition provided a standard but caution not to rely on tradition that has grown tired and corrupt. So, he advocates revitalized and reformed tradition which becomes a moral resource.

Relevance of Gandhian thoughts to Human Resources Development

Gandhian thoughts relating to truth, Dharma, celibacy and non - misappropriation, indeed are not new. He elaborated these abstract principles. Which, since ancient times percolated to present society. Origin of these principles could be found in ancient Indian wisdom, pronounced by sages.

These principles are spelled out in our scriptures. The ancient sages condensed and codified the whole process of human development into "Yama" and "Niyama". Patanjali's Astang Yogasutra is comprehensive treatise on the art of Yoga. Yoga is a system for perfecting human efficiency which simullaneasly corrects the defeets of the body and mind. It invigorates the body, rejuvenate the energies and helps to establish health, happiness, intelligence and reveal full knowledge of self (Sharma , 2006).[8]

The Yoga system contains eight progressive steps such as Yama, Niyama, Asana, Pranayama, Prathihara, Dharna, Dhyana and Samadhi which lead to the ultimate destination of total satisfaction, called *Moksha*. This concept of Moksha is not found in western culture. The first four steps promote physical fitness and control over passions. The last four steps are advanced techniques for mental and spiritual control. Observance of non-violence, truths, non-appropriation, celibacy and detachment are prescribed in Yama.

Niyamas, on the other hand suggest practice to inelucate Yamas in the day-to-day life. These include cleanliness (*Soucha*), contentment (*Santosha*), austerity (*Tapas*), self-study (*Svadhyaya*) and submission of ego (*Ihwara pronidhana*).

Control of desires is essential, say the ancient sages. Passions generate desires and mere satisfaction of desires does not stop recurrence of these desires. Satisfaction multiplies desires, so they are to be controlled by observing Yama and Niyamas.

The implementation of Gandhi's constructive programs on a micro-level basis is taken up by non-government organization, which are volunteree. The average farmers are gradually accepting Gandhi's methods in their lives and economic activities.[13] The central tenets of Gandhi are based on voluntary effort and individual/ community reflections and actions.

Satyagraha, a non-violent and non-cooperative movement started by Gandhi is widely adopted now by people of our country to draw the attention of the polity and force the government to attend to the problems of millions of rural people. Gandhi taught people to protest in a non-violent manner. This vision of Gandhi for/Social clange certainly was set in motion.

Enlightening the rural people for hygienic living be education , training and demonstration in the areas of health, hygiene and eradication of contagions diseases is one way of enlarging the Gandhian ideal of mobilizing the community Creating awareness among people and forming cooperative bodies, clubs or organizations is necessary. Instead of depending on the governmental institutions, the people can be mobilized to build their own roads and drainages for better living conditions.

Planting trees in urban areas is another area for adoption of Gandhi an ideals. The central point is to create awareness among the public and encourage them to put their own efforts for creating a healthy and pleasant environment. This generates communal harmony which Gandhi envisaged in his constructive programmes.

The strategies and philosophy of Gandhi misfired many in other countries. Nelson Mandela in South Africa and Martin Luther king in America working for Civil liberties were the result of Gandhian philosophy and strategy.

Martian Luther king said:

> "If humanity is to progress, Gandhi is inseparable
> He lived throughout and acted , inspired by the vision of
> of humanity evolving towards a world of peace and
> harmony we may ignore
> him at own risk."

REFERENCES

1. Jawaharlal Nehru, (1946), *The Discovery of India.*
2. Hind Swaraj, Ch. 14 as quoted by Ronald in his book Gandhi, p. 22.
3. Gandhi (1946), *Harijan,* Sementer 1946.
4. Iyer (1946), "Writings 2: 262; *Harijan, Modern Review,* October, 1916.
5. Sharma (2006), *Ancient Indian Wisdom is Human Resources Development Personal To-day.* Oct.-Dec., 2006. VII XXVII (3) pp. 26-32.
6. Iyer, *Thought,* 67-68.
7. Iyer, writings (1917), "Satyagraha—Not Previous, Resistance", pp. 44-50.
8. Sharma, C.K. (2006), "Ancient Indian Wisdom in Human Resources Development," pp. 26-32. *Personal Today,* Oct.-Dec., 2006, Vol. XXVIII (3).
9. *Young India,* January 8, 1925.
10. *Young India,* February 5, 1925.
11. Gandhi, M. K. (1958), "All Man are Brothers", ed Krishna Hripalni, New York, Columbia, p. 76.
12. *Harijan,* August 26, 1936.

    Vivek Pinto 1998 " Gandhi is Vision a Values—the Moral Quest for Change in Indian Agriculture," Sage Publications, New Delhi.

4
Sarvodaya Philosophy

Anil Dutta Mishra

Introduction

Sarvodaya, today, does not represent a mere vision or utopian notion but makes an attempt of reorienting human mind to reconstruct human society. It has assumed the dimensions of a movement and a socio-economic force of great potentialities. It is a dynamic philosophy, which can make possible the advent of a radically transformed humanity. Sarvodaya seeks to build a new society on the foundations of old spiritual and moral values of India and attempts to meet the challenge of the contemporary problems.[1] The world has witnessed the propagation, experimentation and implementation of various socio-economic ideologies—capitalist, socialist and communist, time to time. But, in overall consideration, sarvodaya is undoubtedly far more superior to other attributive models. It envisages a well-balanced and integrated development of the nation with no distinction among have and have-nots, privileged and under-privileged, ruler and ruled. The essence of sarvodaya thought lies in socialising matter through the strength of the spirit. Dogmas have no place in sarvodaya, "The philosophy of sarvodaya is not a set of dogmas, in its essence, it is compatible with an attempt of the spirit to prevail over matter and to socialise itself."[2] Sarvodaya is a redeemer's philosophy of social and political orientation, where suffering is, sarvodaya goes to mitigate it. It is the culmination of human emotional integration and the highest intellectual aspiration. It is a symbol of platonic detachment and Gita's Anasakti.[3] It is the highest manifestation of love and attempts at a mental transformation of the people. Gandhi denounced the utilitarian principle of the greatest good of the greatest number, and advocated the sarvodaya philosophy.

Gandhi did not originally coin the word " Sarvodaya". Even before him, the idea of sarvodaya was found in religious books: Vedas, Upanishads, The Ramayan, The Gita, Quran and many others. It was also preached by Indian and Western saints as well as philosophers. But Gandhi gave to these age-old principles and ideals an extended meaning and application. In fact, after the death of Gandhi, the word "Sarvodaya" came into greater prominence, when his fellow-workers assembled at Sevagram (Wardha), in March 1948, and decided to form an organization named 'Sarvodaya Samaj'. This name was chosen in preference to that of 'Satyagraha Mandal' (Satyagraha Circle) because the word 'Satyagraha' had come to acquire a restricted meaning which did not include constructive work. Since then the school of thought which accepts Gandhi's philosophy in all its aspects and of which the central figure is Vinoba Bhave, has come to be known as the 'Sarvodaya School' and its philosophy as the 'Sarvodaya Philosophy'.[4] The prominent thinkers of this school were Acharya Vinoba Bhave, Kishorlal Ghanshyam Mashruwala, J.C. Kumarappa, Kaka Kalelkar, Shankerrao Deo, Dhirendra Mazumdar, Loknayak Jayaprakash Narayan and Acharya J.B. Kripalani. Except Jayaprakash Narayan, all of them had been associated with Gandhi in his constructive work.

Sarvodaya: Meaning and Genesis

'Sarvodaya' is Sanskrit in origin which is comprised of 'Sarva' meaning *all* and 'Udaya' meaning *rising*. The etymological meaning of sarvodaya is the rising of all. This all includes all living beings.[5] In other words, sarvodaya as the word means welfare of all. The word first appeared in the form of the title for the Gujarati translation of John Raskin's book entitled 'Unto this Last'.[6] Sarvodaya was the title of series of nine articles, which Gandhi wrote and got published in Gujarati in the *Indian Opinion* weekly in South Africa in 1908.[7]

Sarvodaya is essentially a spiritual activity, which has two meanings, viz., negative and positive. As a negative concept, Sarvodaya is not limited to one person or to one group of persons. Nobody is excluded from enjoying anything from others.[8] It is not something which one man or set of men can gain or enjoy to the exclusion of others.[9] As a positive concept, Sarvodaya implies the participation of all kinds of people irrespective of class, caste, creed and religion. It also stands for the total blossoming of all the faculties – physical, mental and spiritual of the human being. It is an activity in which all may partake and if it is to amount to a full realization of the human faculties of the human soul. [10]

According to Acharya Vinoba Bhave, the term Sarvodaya commands a two-fold meaning. Firstly, Sarvodaya means making all happy by removing suffering and poverty with the help of scientific knowledge. Secondly, establishing a world state full with divinity, kindness and equality is called Sarvodaya. [11] Sarvodaya aims not at the rise of the few or the many, or for that matter the rise of the greatest number. It is not utilitarianism, which stands for the greatest good of the greatest number. It contains the germ of minority and majority. Contrary to utilitarianism stands for the good of one and all, of the high and the low, of the strong and the weak, the intelligent as well as the dull. As against the Laissez -faire theory, that is the survival of the fittest, Sarvodaya believes in the survival and development of all. To Vinoba, "The idea of Sarvodaya, as preached by the Gita is to merge oneself in the good of all." [12]

Apart from connoting the welfare of all, Sarvodaya commands two more meanings, firstly, the universal welfare and secondly, the integrated development of all. The laissez-faire philosophy stands for the exploitation of many by a few. The utilitarian school supports the majority, totally neglecting the minority. Sarvodaya rejects these theories, which stand for the joy of few, advocates the welfare of all, irrespective of class, costs, creed, colour, race, region or religion. The philosophy of Sarvodaya makes the attempt or reorienting human mind, of reconstructing human society. It means welfare and prosperity of all. All must progress together without collision of interest.[13] Interpreting the purport of Sarvodaya, Dada Dharmadhikari said: "Sarvodaya is a term with a wider connotation since it conceives of assimilation of all and not only of many or most.[14] Sarvodaya is a philosophy, which provides checks against the imperfections of human mind and soul.

As regards the meaning of the word "Sarvodaya", there are broadly two views: the first, in its micro-form, means simply the rise of one and all; secondly, the macro-form connotes the rise of all, the universal welfare and the all round development of all.[15] But it connotes several other meanings. In its negative sense, it never omits even a singly person from enjoying anything from the rest of the mankind. As a positive concept, it promotes the development of all the faculties of man. According to Vinoba Bhave, it stands for not only making all happy by eliminating suffering from all but also for bringing a world state based on equality. For Gandhi, Sarvodaya as a broader concept stands for the merger of one in all with self-sacrifice and a selfless service. It aims at not only fulfilling the minimum material needs but also developing the ethico -spiritual aspects of all people.

Sources of Sarvodaya

The following sources helped Gandhi to develop his concept of Sarvodaya. These were—Ruskin's book *Unto This Last,* Tolstoy's *The Kingdom of God is Within You,* Thoreau's *Civil Disobedience,* The Bhagvad Gita, Isavayopanisad, Buddhism, Jainism and Islam.

Ruskin's 'Unto This Last'

The Gandhian philosophy of Sarvodaya can be traced to the central teachings of India's spiritual and religious heritage although Gandhi admits the fact that he had immediate inspiration from Ruskin's *Unto This Last* of which the term Sarvodaya is his rendering.[16] The welfare of all became the basic idea of Gandhi's philosophy right from the days when he wrote in Gujarati his most world famous thirty thousand words book *Hind Swaraj or Indian Home Rule* in 1909.

Gandhi called one of the chapters of his Autobiography *The Magic Spell of Book* wherein he describes the effects of Ruskin's *Unto This Last* (meaning uplift of the last). He translated it later into Gujarati claiming it Sarvodaya. It is a book from which Gandhi drew great inspiration and he at once determined to change his view of life in line with the ideals embodied in Ruskin's book *Unto This Last.*[17]

The central teaching of *Unto This Last,* according to Gandhi are:

That the good of the individual is contained in the good of all.

That a lawyer's work has the same values as the Barber's in as much as all have the same right of earning their livelihood from their work.

That a life of labour, i.e., the life of the tiller of the soil and the handicraftsman is the life worth living.

There is a controversy with regard to the meanings of the terms "Unto This Last" and "Sarvodaya". Gandhi himself acknowledged that he translated it later into Gujrati, entitling it Sarvodaya. On the one hand, Benudhar Pradhan opines that the idea of welfare of all formed a part of his mental make-up even before he read this book.[18] This view is further strengthened from what Gandhi has expressed in his own words – "The first of these I knew"[19] On the other hand, Geoffery Ashe doubted whether the idea of Sarvodaya is contained at all in Ruskin's *Unto This Last*. Persons like Benudhar affirms that "it will be a travesty of truth to say that the objective of 'welfare of all' does not remain couched in the pages of *Unto This Last* of Ruskin."[20]

Ruskin and Gandhi both, were earnestly concerned with social welfare. While Ruskin aimed at the social welfare of 'the greatest number', Gandhi aimed at the welfare of all. Therefore, Vinobha Bhave feels that Gandhi is the real author of the term Sarvodaya, since the term, 'Unto This Last' would mean only the uplift of the last (*Antyodaya*). In fact, one has to accept that Ruskin's Unto This Last had directly or indirectly had a profound influence on Gandhi in fulfilling the ideal of Sarvodaya, which he had already cherished as his life's mission.

Leo Tolstoy's 'The Kingdom of God is Within You'

Gandhi was greatly influenced by Leo Tolstoy, through his book *The Kingdom of God is Within You* and his essay on 'Christianity and Patriotism'. Tolstoy's simplicity of life and purity of purpose influenced Gandhi deeply. His views on Christianity, its church, its teachings roused Gandhi's feelings. Tolstoy accepted love to be the law of life. The principles of non-violence, is based on love for the entire mankind. Tolstoy and Gandhi, both adopted the instrument of love to solve all problems in their lives. In his celebrated book *The Kingdom of God is Within You*, we find a political force creating an indelible mark on Gandhi. Gandhi confessed that its reading cured him of the skepticism and made him a firm believer of Ahimsa. Both Tolstoy and Gandhi firmly believed that non-violence could cure all social maladies, remove political ills, and establish peace on the earth and goodwill among mankind. In fact, both Tolstoy and Gandhi believed in the efficacy of love for the cure of evil and suffering in this world. Tolstoy perceived the truth, love and non-violence and Gandhi grasped the essence of these virtues and led his life directed towards these paths.[21]

Tolstoy also impressed upon Gandhi's mind the importance of bread-labour. For Tolstoy, the man who abstains from manual labour is a thief of the society. Gandhi acknowledged his debt to Tolstoy. He says, "the law that to live man must work, first come home to me upon reading Tolstoy's writing, 'On Bread Labour' – only those man deserve to eat bread who actually till the ground, spin cloth and produce things'. Tolstoy says, 'let us get off the shoulder of our neighbours' and Gandhi adds that if everyone performed that simple operation, he would have rendered all service God requires of him. Since every man has an obligation to himself as well as to the society, bread labour becomes an imperative duty which must be performed by each and every man.[22]

Gandhian philosophy of Sarvodaya comes very close to Tolstoyan philosophy of anarchism. The pure ideal of Gandhi's conception of Sarvodaya is an ideal of philosophical anarchism, a stateless society marked by voluntary co-operation. Profound faith in God, commiseration from the exploited, inherent aversion to violence, deep-rooted belief in the dignity of man led the two philosophers to the same goal and objective. But Gandhi is not a through-going Tolstoyan. The difference between the two philosophers arises out of the fact that Gandhi is far more practical than Tolstoy. Tolstoy recoils from all expressions of violence. Gandhi permits violence, provided of course, that motive for violence is not anger but true love. Thus the moral content of Gandhi's doctrine of Ahimsa, which forms the fulcrum around which the entire doctrine of Sarvodaya ideology is based, has a higher significance than that of Tolstoy's. This is due to the fact that Gandhi was greatly influenced by the Gita ideal of *niskamakarma,* i.e. action without attachment.[23]

Thoreau's 'Civil Disobedience'

The American pacifist Thoreau was the champion of the free sprit and was repelled by the established political and economic routine of time. In him we discover an element of moral individualism culminating in his concept of 'civil disobedience'. Thoreau used the term in his speeches in 1849. It is obvious that Gandhi did not derive his idea of 'civil disobedience' from the writings of Thoreau. In fact, the resistance to authority in South Africa preceded before Gandhi got the essay of Thoreau on 'civil disobedience'. This movement was then known as 'passive resistance'. Gandhi was not satisfied with the term 'civil disobedience' because it failed to convey the full meaning of the struggle. Hence, he adopted the phrase 'civil resistance.'[24]

Thoreau did not believe in narrow sectarianism and felt that man is meant to experience God, not to theologies about him. Man according to Thoreau is a social being who is generally disposed to co-operation with fellow beings for social good. He felt that the moral institutions of the state supported by coercive authority hamper the individual's moral and spiritual freedom. He, therefore, visualised a society in which government will disappear. 'That Government is best which governs not at all', or, 'which governs least'. Like Thoreau, Gandhi also held that the democracy could be realized only in a stabilize society based on Truth and Non-violence. And Gandhi described it as Sarvodaya, which promotes not only social welfare but spiritual upliftment. Thus Gandhi heard an echo of his own thought in Thoreau.[25]

The Bhagavad Gita

Gandhi drew his primary strength and inspiration from the Bhagvad Gita. To Gandhi, the Gita is the 'Eternal Mother'. According to him, the theme of Gita is self-realization. He says: "self-realization and its means is the theme of the Gita."[26] Again he affirms, "to one who reads the spirit of the Gita, it teaches the secret of non-violence the secret of realizing the self through the physical body."[27]

The sole aim of the Gita is to suppress unrighteousness and to establish Dharma. It wants to bring prosperity and peace to all. It presents in concise form the Hindu view of life, which in turn stands for the universal brotherhood of all beings. It also highlights the importance of all selfless service for the promotion of the welfare of the whole creation since God and the creation is one. Through Svadharma, the Gita aims at 'Sarvabhutahita' or the good of all beings.[28] In this way, Gita preaches the message of the welfare of all or Sarvodaya, which influenced Gandhi's thought, and action.

Isavayopanisad

The first verse of Isavayopanisad deals with the ideology of Sarvodaya. The first part of the verse contains the principles of equality and fraternity. And the second part reveals the ideas of renunciation, non-acquisitiveness, non-exploitation and service to the society. According to Gandhi, since the entire universe is pervaded by God, the verse preaches the philosophy of equality and fraternity, which are the fundamental principles of the welfare of all. He confirms, "Universal brotherhood not only brotherhood of all human beings but of all living beings, I find in this mantra..."[29]

Buddhism

According to Lord Buddha, all life is suffering. Suffering has to be extirepated in order to enjoy the bliss of nirvana, which is the highest goal in Buddhism. Nirvana is both individualistic and universal or cosmic. It may be realized in his life, here and there. It may also be known as full and perfect enlightenment for the sake of all beings. All can obtain nirvana if they meticulously follow the Noble Eight-Fold Path of Buddha. Gandhi was highly influenced and deeply impressed by the Buddhist philosophy, which preached universal love, non-injury to living beings, sacrifice and renunciation for the sake of promoting the welfare of all. The Buddha stressed on purity of means, which in turn influenced Gandhi who constantly maintained that there is indissoluble relationship between pure means and noble end.[30] Buddha preached about the middle path. Similarly, in Sarvodaya, it is understood that no one should take extreme step.

Jainism

The ideal of the welfare of all forms is the corner stone of the Jainism. Ahimsa forms one of the five vows. The positive aspect of non-violence is the love for fellow beings, not only human but also all creatures. A Jain Tirthankara's duty is to devote his whole life for showering happiness on all the beings of the whole universe. About the place of Sarvodaya in Jainism, Binudhar Pradhan states: "The concept of welfare of all was so much an integral part of Jaina philosophy that the term 'Sarvodaya' was used by one Jaina teacher Samantabhadra even before the Christian era."[31] Further, Benudhar Pradhan argues that though the word 'Sarvodaya' is used by the Jaina Saint Samantabhadra for the first time, yet Gandhi's use of the word is completely his own. According to him, the term Sarvodaya came to Gandhi "as if in a flash."[32] Therefore, he maintains that "the word Sarvodaya ... was purely his own coinage."[33]

Islam

Gandhi had a great respect for Islam. He learnt the message of universal brotherhood from it. As for Islam, Gandhi declares that in his view, 'the point of brotherhood is manifested in no other religion as clearly as in Islam'. The reading of the holy Koran convinced Gandhi that the basis of Islam is not violence.[34] In fact, Gandhi shows remarkable catholicity and sympathetic and reverential attitude towards all religions of the world.

Apart from *Unto This Last, The Kingdom of God is Within You*, the Upanishads, the Gita, Buddhism and Jainism, Gandhia's concept of Sarvodaya was also influenced by Vaishnavism, Zorostrianism and Christianity. The revival of the ancient teachings by Gandhi and incorporating them in his philosophy of Sarvodaya is perhaps his greatest contribution to the world of thought. Gandhi attempted the synthesis of the ideas of Vedanta, Buddhism, Jainism, Christianity and the teaching of prophets like Tulsidas, Tolstoy, Thoreau, Ruskin and national leaders of the Indian Renaissance movement. The philosophy of Sarvodaya takes up the Gandhian synthesis and tries to work out the implication of their ideas at more critical and analytical levels.[35]

Ends and Means in Sarvodaya

Morality is the essential means to achieve spirituality and good society or good ends. But communists like Machiavelli maintain that end justifies the means. This reveals that through any impure means like cunning, hypocrisy, hatred or violence one can get one's own desired end. To them, ends and means are watertight compartment. End is everything, no matter what or how the means are. Means become good if they serve the end. Jayaprakash. Narayan observed impartially: "In Marxism any means are good means provided they serve the ends of the social revolution."[36]

For Gandhi means determine the end. He says, "As the means so the end."[37] Means are as important as the ends. "In a way, his unique contribution to the world lies in his maintaining that the means are more important than the ends."[38] His emphasis on means rather than on the end is based on the doctrine of *niskamakarma* which holds that a person can have control over actions and not on their fruit. Gandhi is fully convinced that man can only strive but cannot command results. He maintains that "means are after all everything. There is no wall of separation between means and ends. Indeed the creator gives us control over means, none over the end. Realization of the goal is in exact proportion to that of the means. This is a proportion that admits of no exception."[39] Gandhi stress on the strength of the means is based on the following reasons: *(i)* He believes in the progressive evolution of man; *(ii)* He fixes the end of man as self-perfection; *(iii)* He feels that the end is always out of man's grip till it is attained; and *(iv)* He is convinced that if means are subordinated to ends, the ends to which means are subordinated are likely to be less effective. All the above conviction made Gandhi to held the view that man must have complete control over means, despite both means and ends are various and contradictory.[40]

According to Gandhi, the end justifying the means is dangerous in practice and unsound ethically. If it is accepted, it permits resource to violence, fraud, untruth, opportunism etc. Gandhi viewed human beings as supreme. They are ends in themselves. If the means are pure, the end also becomes pure. When we take care of the means, the end will take care of itself.[41] By emphasizing only the means, Gandhi does not intend to give a secondary place to the ends. To him, means and ends are inseparably connected just like seed and trees are connected.[42]

By considering means and ends as a continuous process, Gandhi dissolved the age-old opinion of viewing both as water-tight compartments. The difference between them is imaginary.[43] Therefore, he takes them as an organic whole. In a way, he proposes that both means and end must be homogeneous. He also holds that the extreme of means is itself the end. That is, the end progressively realizes itself through the means. The end can never result all of a sudden out of the means. In fact, when means slowly progresses, it turns itself into the end. The means apart from leading to an end shapes the end. In Gandhian philosophy, self-realization or spiritual freedom is the end of all human actions. Gandhi throughout his life tirelessly tried to use sarvodaya social order as the means to achieve spiritual freedom. Sarvodaya society guarantees moral freedom to every individual. This moral freedom, in turn, progresses itself into spiritual freedom, when it is followed meticulously placing faith in the supremacy of God. Moral freedom as means and spiritual freedom as end forms a continuous process or organic wholes. They cannot be divided into water- tight compartments. Their difference is only imaginary. Both are convertible terms. That is what Gandhi too reveals. What is needed is understanding and practicing ethics as god has given. Sarvodaya, as it enjoys ethico-spiritual basis, it can also be equitable both moral freedom and spiritual freedom. Thus, the problem of ends and means, as an organic whole, occupies a unique place in Gandhian thought, contributing to sarvodaya, moral freedom, spiritual freedom, political freedom and spiritual economic freedom.

Sarvodaya Social Order

Gandhi with his many-sided personality had a clear vision and definite approach to the problems, which faced India of his time. Indian society was full with deep-rooted evils. It had totally degenerated itself socially, politically, economically and educationally. Penury had further ruined India social conditions which were already corroded with caste-conflicts, child-marriages, untouchability, Sati, Pardah, negation of education to women, dowry, polygamy, corruption, exploitation, etc. Gandhi tried to find immediate solutions to all these problems.[44]

In sarvodaya society, there is no scope for exploitation, discrimination, inequality and violence. Gandhi[45] envisaged that sarvodaya society should also be free from evils like 'politics without principle', 'wealth without work', 'knowledge without character', 'commerce without morals', 'science without mankind' and 'service without scarifies'. It should not be divided into watertight compartments called social, political and religious where all these act and react upon one another. His aim of sarvodaya made him to establish a close correlation among these problems. The sarvodaya society is an indivisible whole. In order to establish a democratic and free society Gandhi suggested every individual to imbibe the spirit of love, tolerance, kindness, fearlessness, non-violence etc. A non-violent society, however small it is, is the strongest one. Non-violence as the law of life includes individuals, societies and nations. To him, non-violence is both a personal and social virtue. A society built on the basis of complete Ahimsa is the purest anarchy.[46]

For Sarvodaya mentality, certain attributes are essential. Gandhi has offered the 'eleven vows' to discipline oneself so that a disciplined society could emerge. Self-scarifie is the essence of

Sarvodaya social order. Every individual is to be ready and willing to sacrifice his happiness for the sake of others. Everyone is to follow the policy of giving and not taking. He is to work for others and not expect anything in return for the same. Through Sarvodaya he wanted to rebuild the nation "from the bottom-up-wards" and establish a new social order based on freedom, justice, equality and fraternity. Gandhi's ideal (Sarvodaya) society will be marked by following characteristics:[47]

There should be no coercive state power in it and social cohesion should be maintained through the citizens' sense of social obligation like the obligations of Varnashram dharma in ancient India.

It should consist of villages or rural agricultural settlements in which wants are few and co-operation, conservation and decentralization are the governing norms of social, civil and economic activity.

Besides agriculture, other production should be based on cottage industries and handicraft. Even education should be handicraft-centered.

The ruling principles of decentralized and handicraft-centered production, three other economic norms should be maintained or practiced, namely, village self-sufficiency, bread-labour (i.e. winning one's bread through work done by one's own body labour), and non-possession (acquiring or using the minimum possible articles of consumption). Heavy machines and heavy transport will have no place in this society.

In such a society, disputes or conflict (generally arising out of the craze for power, property or possession) will be few and for between. But in order to deal with such disputes, as may possibly or occasionally arise, village panchayats should be organised. In the unlikely event of the failure of panchayats, recourse may be had to Satyagraha.

Gandhi had set-up his first sarvodaya community on a farm near Durban and called it Phoenix (c. 1904), followed by another one (C. 1910) over Johannesburg named after Leo Tolstoy. The idea behind these two settlements was that the inmates had to perform all chores of running the farms, whatever is their avocation, on living wages, so that they become self-reliant and self-sufficient. In fact, through the pursuit of sarvodaya ideals, Gandhi wanted to chart out an alternative course. The ideas on sarvodaya social order find their fullest expression in his constructive work programme that began to unfold itself on his arrival in India from South Africa. Khadi, Communal amity, removal of untouchability, promotion of village industries, village sanitation, basic education, etc., came one after another and so did the supporting organization. Some of these organisation were: All India Spinners Association, All India Harijan Sewak Sangh, Hindustani Prachar Sabha, Hindustan Talimi Sangh and Akhil Bharat Sewa Sangh. The sarvodaya society is an ideal society and an ideal cannot be fully realized. Gandhi also believed that an ideal is never fully realized in life."[48]

Sarvodaya Political Order

Sarvodaya as a political doctrine is mildly anarchist. In fact, the political ideal of Sarvodaya is an anarchism of its own variety. It concedes that a fully stateless society is beyond the reach of man, and the goal of human endeavour can only be to reduce the power and sphere of the state to the minimum. The politics of sarvodaya is politics of Lokniti instead of *rajniti*. *Lokniti* is a comprehensive term, which denotes simultaneously a way of life a form of social order and a method. As a way of life, it stands for the self-regulation of individual conduct and for a habit to act on one's own initiatives. As a form of social order, it envisages a society in which police and military will have little to do and the law will interfere, least with life. A man will have the utmost freedom of action. As a method, it stands for social change in a manner that would maintain men's freedom of action.[49] The Sarvodaya Political order is based on certain fundamental political assumptions:

All individuals are equally born.

People are the custodians of the supreme power in the State.

Political power should be decentralized both at individual and the village level.

All must train themselves for self-rule.

All should believe in the divinity of every individual and strive for the welfare of all people.[50]

The ultimate goal for Gandhi is the greatest good of all people. Good, to him, means only the self-realization but not the material well-being of the individuals or the society. A study on the nature of sarvodaya political order demands a brief survey of his view on State, Swaraj, Satyagraha, Democracy, Nationalism, Internationalism and Ram Rajya.[51]

According to Vinoba Bhave,[52] there are ten criteria of an ideal polity:

1. International fraternity.
2. The conscious, spontaneous (as far as possible) and hearty co-operation of all the inhabitants of the country.
3. The identity of the good of the capable minority and the general majority.
4. The orientation towards the universal and equal development of all.
5. The widest dispersion of political sovereignty.
6. The least amount of government.
7. The easiest availability of tantra or justice (?) – (*Sulabhatama tantra*).
8. The least possible expenditure.
9. The lowest degree of external protection.
10. One universal, uninterrupted, and neutral or objective spread of knowledge.

Sarvodaya Economic Order

Gandhi adopted an integral approach to human problems. His basic aim was to reduce economics to terms of religion and spirituality. For him, ethics and economics are not two different entities. Economics that hurt the moral well-being of an individual or a nation are immoral and therefore sinful.[53] True economics, according to Gandhi "stands for social justice, it promotes the good of all equally including the weakest and is indispensable for decent life."[54] He mainly wants to formulate such an economic constitution to both India and the World that no one suffer from want of food, clothing and shelter. All necessities of life "should be freely available to all as God's air and water are or ought to be –."[55] Such an economic constitution, he aims at building not on material wealth but on spirituality. This is only possible when everyone shows more truth than gold, greater fearlessness than pomp of power and wealth, greater charity than love of self.

The Gandhian Sarvodaya economic order is based on simplicity, decentralization, self-sufficiency, co-operation, equality, non-violence, sanctity of labour, human values, self-sufficient village units, nationalization of basic industries, swadeshi, and the theory of trusteeship. These, in turn, will solve the problems pertaining to labour, capital, production, distribution and profit etc.

In the Gandhian economic order, dependence on others is slavery and self-sufficiency is freedom. Regional self-sufficiency is must in Sarvodaya economic order. People should produce their own needs of life. Production must be in accordance with the need.

In the Sarvodaya economic order, man is totally free from material bondage. He never becomes a slave to material wants. He lives above his greed and amassing of riches. He views work as service. It is divine for him. He cherishes the principles of self-suffering, sacrifice, dedication and renunciation. His eating, clothing or dwelling shows no superiority or inferiority. He finds no difference between the rich and the poor. Really Sarvodaya economic system is practical, realistic and humane.

Socialism, Communism and Sarvodaya

Gandhi called himself a socialist and even a communist but for him socialism and communism were transcendental forms of egalitarian social philosophy that find their fulfillment and culmination in Sarvodaya.[56] Although the situational background from which socialism and Sarvodaya have emerged is different, still their humanist idealism is almost similar.[57] According to Jayaprakash Narayan, Sarvodaya represents the highest socialist values. Socialism arose in the west as a philosophy of the industrial proletariat and challenged the pretensions of the contemporary state, which bolstered the interests of the capitalists.[58]

Socialism and communism are basically idealistic, ethical and humanitarian in nature. They are concerned with the illumination of the misery of the millions, elevation of the status of poor, unfortunate and downtrodden and founding a society based on the principle of economic equality and social justice. Sarvodaya stand for the just society free from all types of exploitation and human miseries. According to Rajendra Prasad,[59] Sarvodaya represents an aspiration "towards a society based on truth and non-violence in which there will be no distinction of caste or creed, no opportunity for exploitation and full scope for development both for individuals as well as groups." Jayaprakash Narayan[60] writes about Sarvodaya, "What we desire is the establishment of a society in which there will be no exploitation, there will be perfect equality and each individual will have equal opportunities for development."[61] Sarvodaya aims at a "classless, casteless and non-exploitative society."[62] Vinoba[63] said "There is no permanent conflict between the two ideologies-Marxism and Sarvodaya. Whatever differences there might be between Gandhism and communism, there are also points of similarity between these and these too are important. The cause of the have-nots is the basic sentiment running through both. Both Ganhism and communism regard the well-being of the poor and the oppressed with the intensely loving regard of the Mother." K.G. Mashruwala, prominent Gandhian observes, "the common point between Gandhi and Marx is the extreme concern of both for the suppressed and the oppressed, the resourceless and the ignorant, the dumb and starving section of humanity." Similarly, Jayaprakash Narayan[64] said, "If we are true socialists, we would be true follower of sarvodaya as well."

In spite of some fundamental similarities between socialism and sarvodaya, there is great differences between them on the question of means and methods. From the sarvodaya stand point; there are two shortcomings in the socialist philosophy. First, the basic technique for effectuating socialism is supposed to be nationalization. But nationalization may entrench the control of the bureaucrats and may be another name for state capitalism. According to sarvodaya, the socialist belief in positive state action as the sovereign remedy for human ills is unfounded. Sarvodaya pleads for villagization while socialism believes in nationalization, sarvodaya accepts village ownership. Secondly, socialism adheres, at least in some cases, to the concept of violent revolution. But sarvodaya has no place for violence in its philosophy and technique.[65]

The difference between sarvodaya and communism are far more basic and fundamental. Communism advocates a violent technique for a change over in favour of egalitarian society, a society free form exploitation and privilege. Sarvodaya, to the contrary believes in persuasion and change of heart. Both Marx and Engels expressed their conviction that "violent overthrow of the bourgeoisie lays the foundation for the sway of the proletariat." Lenin and Mao used the technique of violence to bring about a change in the Soviet Union and China respectively. While Gandhi has taught the ethics of self-suffering to convert the opponent because violence can never be the foundation of a just and equal society.[66] Violence breeds counter-violence. And on the basis of violence it is not possible to establish the just social order. In fact a new form of exploitation of man has come into existence and that is exploitation by the party bosses, bureaucrats and the state machine.

The Sarvodaya avoids the evils of legislative or legal coercion in democratic socialism and violence and physical coercion involved in communism. It relies on the technique of conversion for bringing about social transformation in the direction of a non-exploitative and egalitarian society. Gandhi was concerned with the welfare of all and hence rejected the view that the welfare of all can ever be attained by physical, intellectual and moral coercion perpetrated by a section of the people against the rest of the community. Gandhiji believed that sarvodaya could be realised only by the application of a moral and ethical method. Gandhi believed that through the application of the technique of persuasion and appeal to the innate good sense of the rich and the privileged, they might be made to renounce their privileges and apply their superfluous wealth for the welfare of the community. Such renunciation of wealth and privilege was to be for the good of the poor and the rich. "The essence of the revolution contemplated by sarvodaya is that it plans its faith on human approach, at the root of which stands the concept of revolution by human beings for the proliferation of human values and human virtues, and through a method that is strictly humane."[67]

The advocates of Sarvodaya also differ from the communists and socialists in respect of the role of the state. Both the communists and the socialists have their faith in the potency of the state to bring about equality in society. In the economic sphere, the communists and socialists advocate centralization and concentration of economic powers in the hands of the state and the proliferation of the economic activities of the state. To quote Japrakash Narayan:[68] "Democratic socialists, communists as well as welfarists are all statists." The concentration of both political and economic power in the hands of the state leads to too much of bureaucratisation, dehumanisation and loss of individual freedom. To quote Jayaprakash Narayan: [69] "The democratic state remains a Leviathan that will sit heavily on the freedom of the people." The state is still worse under communism. It is true that the communists talk about the withering away of the state in the long run, but during the transitional period, the state is not only tolerated but also becomes more and more powerful. It devours the lofty ideals of classless society-liberty, equality, fraternity and fellowship. Jayaprakash Narayan writes, "The remedy is to create and develop forms of socialist living through the voluntary endeavour of the people rather than seek to establish socialism by the use of the power of the state. In other words, the remedy is to establish people's socialism, rather than state socialism."[70]

Considering from all angles, Sarvodaya is a far nobler, subtler, loftier, broader, deeper and transcendental concept than socialism or communism. According to Vinobaji, "Sarvodaya is a better word than 'socialist'; it is also our own native word, born from our own soil and carrying a noble meaning. We do not use the word because we are a little doubtful if we can live up to it. So we prefer the world 'socialist'. But our goal is in fact sarvodaya and our people are being prepared for absorption into the sea of sarvodaya." It is true that socialism and communism can realise their true meaning and fulfil their objective by merging their identity with sarvodaya. Jayaprakash Narayan[71] writes: "Socialism as we understand it today, cannot take mankind to the sublime goals of freedom, equality, brotherhood and peace. Socialism no doubt gives promise to bring mankind closer to those goals than any other competing social philosophy. But I am persuaded that unless socialism is transformed into sarvodaya, those goals would remain beyond its reach. Vinoba writes, "There is no permanent conflict between the two ideologies—Marxism and Sarvodaya. As the Ganges becomes wider and wider and moves on and finally merges in the ocean, I hope Marxism will merge in Sarvodaya one day."[72]

Sarvodaya and Contemporary Crisis

The Sarvodaya principles are capable of meeting the greatest challenge of the age. The most urgent need of today is the abolition of human suffering as well as of war. Even Sarvodaya will be very important in 21st Century due to complexity of human behaviour. Sarvodaya by laying stress on the goodness of human nature, unity of mankind, service of man, application of moral principles considered valid for individuals to group life and inter-state relations, the non-violent process of change, social and economic equality, economic and political decentralization, tries to resolve the various kinds of tensions that disturb domestic and international harmony. Sarvodaya is capable of strengthening the forces of love, creativeness and joy of life. Sarvodaya takes a whole view of man and emphasizes his spiritual nature. In modern context the concept of sarvodaya can be interpreted as the "awakening of one and all." Thus, in addition to the awakening of everyone, it refers to the awakening of the total human spirit and personality. Sarvodaya is also related to achieving the highest level of self-realization in which one sees one's manifestation in all others.

Our political, social and economic life has been sized with a malady. The malady of our times perhaps of all times, is mad quest for power, whether it is political, social or economic. Service is being given up in quest of personal aggrandisement. Humanity is undergoing almost a phase of moral collapse and ethical nihilism. In the era of the mad rush for power, the significance of Sarvodaya lies in stressing the permanent value of self-abnegation. Sarvodaya is giving expression to a moral principle of cardinal importance because it wants to enshrine the primacy of goodness and character in place of the skill of manipulation and self-assertion. Sarvodaya appeals to the mind and heart in terms of values and goals. The decadence and corruption, which in fact organized institutional mechanism, can be removed only by the reassertion of moral and spiritual values and their ever-growing incorporation in social, political and economic life. Sarvodaya is the only way to solve the problems of unemployment, unequal distribution of wealth, growing corruption in public life etc. The moral collapse and prostration of our world needs the revitalizing notion of ethical idealism and stress on the moral approach to social and economic problems, which sarvodaya envisages.

Summing up

Sarvodaya philosophy, based on the insights and experiences of Gandhi, is a reassertion of the valuation and moral approach to the problems of mankind, which has been a part of ancient Indian culture for ages. Vinoba Bhave rightly said, "Sarvodaya stands for not only making all happy by illuminating suffering from all but also for bringing a world state based on equality."[73] For Gandhi, sarvodaya stands for the merger of one in all with self-sacrifice and a selfless service. His Sarvodaya ideal, apart from standing for the meaning of the welfare of all, implies the meaning of the universal welfare and integrated development of all. As a universal ideal, it aims at not only fulfilling the minimum material needs but also developing the ethico-spiritual aspects of all people. The great contribution of Sarvodaya in the present century lies in the reassertion of the Gandhian moral approach to the problems of mankind and a vision that looks forward to the creation of a welfare state and society.

REFERENCES

1. V. P. Verma, *The Political Philosophy of Mahatma Gandhi and Sarvodaya*, Lakshmi Naryan Agarwal, Agra, 1980, 4th Edition, p. 279.
2. J.N. Mohanty, "Sarvodaya and Aurobindo—a Rapprochement", Gandhi Marg, Vol. 4, No. 30, July 1960, p. 211.
3. B.P. Pandey, *Gandhi, Sarvodaya and Organizations*, Chugh Publications, Allahabad, 1988, pp. 20-21.
4. Vishwanath Tandon, *The Social and Political Philosophy of Sarvodaya After Gandhi*, Sarva Seva Sangh Prakashan, Varanasi, 1965, p. 2.
5. Anil Dutta Mishra, *Fundamentals of Gandhism*, Mittal Publications, New Delhi, 1995, p. 5.
6. Mahajan, P. Mani and K.S. Bharathi, *Foundations of Gandhian Thought*, Dattsons, Nagpur, 1987, p. 68.
7. *The Collected Works of Mahatama Gandhi*, Vol. 8., Publications Division, Government of India, New Delhi,1962, pp. 239-41.
8. K.M. Rathnam Chetty, *Sarvodaya and Freedom: A Gandhian Appraisal, Discovery* Publishing House, New Delhi, 1991, p. 46.
9. B.S. Sharma, "The Philosophical Basis of Sarvodaya", Gandhi Marg, vol. 4, No. 3, July 1960, p. 259.
10. *Ibid.*
11. K.M. Rathnam Chetty, *op.cit.*, p. 47.
12. *Harijan*, 13.2.1949.
13. B. P. Pandey, *op. cit.*, p. 14.
14. Dada Dharmadhikari, *Sarvodaya Darshan*, Sarva Seva Sangh Prakashan, Varanasi, p. 18.
15. K.M. Rathnam Chetty, *op. cit.*, p. 48.
16. *Ibid.*, p. 38.
17. *Ibid.*
18. Benudhar Pradhan, *The Socialist Thought of Mahatma Gandhi*, G.D.K. Publications, Delhi, 1980, Vol. I, p. 284.

19. M.K. Gandhi, *An Autobiography The Story of my Experiments with Truth,* Navjivan Publishing House, Ahmadabad,1948, p. 365.
20. Benudhar Pradhan, *op. cit,* p. 285.
21. K.M. Rathnam Chetty, *op. cit.,* pp. 39-40.
22. *Ibid.,* p. 40.
23. *Ibid.,* pp. 40-41.
24. *Ibid.,* p. 41.
25. *Ibid.*
26. M.K. Gandhi, *Young India,* 12-11-1925.
27. *Ibid.*
28. K.M. Rathanaim Chetty, *op.cit.,* pp. 42-43.
29. Anil Dutta Mishra, *op.cit.,* p. 11.
30. *Ibid.* p. 11
31. Benudhar Pradhan, *op.cit.,* p. 294.
32. *Ibid.,* p. 301.
33. *Ibid.,* p. 302.
34. K.M. Rathnam Chetty *op.cit.,* p. 45.
35. *Ibid.*
36. Jayaprakash Narayan, *Socialism, Sarvodaya and Communism,* A.P.H. Bombay, 1964, p. 149.
37. M.K. Gandhi, *Young India,* p. 364.
38. S. Gopalan, *Means and ends: The Gandhian View,* Gandhi Centenary Volume, 1969, p. 70.
39. M.K. Gandhi, *Young India,* 17.7.1924.
40. D.G. Tendulkar, *Mahatma,* Vol. II, New Delhi, Publications Division, 1951, p. 299.
41. M.K. Gandhi, *Harijan,* 27.2.1949.
42. M.K.Gandhi, *Hind Swaraj or Indian Home Rule,* Ahmedabad, Navajivan Publishing House, 1946, p. 60.
43. *Harijan,* 27 February 1949.
44. A. D. Mishra, *op.cit,* p. 14.
45. *Ibid.*
46. *Ibid.,* p. 15.
47. S.C. Gangal, *Gandhian Thought and Techniques in the Modern World,* Criterion Publications, New Delhi, 1988, pp. 158-59.
48. *Ibid.,* p. 159.
49. Vishwanath Tandon, *op.cit.,* pp. 124-25.
50. K.M. Rathnam Chetty, *op.cit.,* p. 66.
51. Anil Dutta Mishra, *op.cit.,* pp. 16-17.
52. V.P.Varma, *The Political Philosophy of Mahatma Gandhi and Sarvodaya,* Agra, Lakshmi Narayan agarwal, 1980, p. 295.
53. N.K. Bose, *Selection From Gandhi,* Navjivan Publishing House, Ahmedabad, 1994, p. 40.
54. *Harijan,* 9 October,1937.

55. Young India,15 July 1928.
56. V.D. Mahajan, *Modern Indian Political Thought*, p. 569.
57. Jayaprakash Narayan, *From Socialism to Sarvodaya*, Madras, Socialist Book Centre, 1956, p. 96.
58. V.P. Varma, *op.cit.*, p. 283.
59. V.D.Mahajan, *op.cit.* p. 569.
60. *Ibid.*
61. *Ibid.*, pp. 569-70.
62. *Ibid.*, p. 570.
63. *Ibid.*
64. *Ibid.*
65. V.P. Varma, *op.cit.*, p. 285.
66. Vibona Bhave, *Swarajya Shastra*, New Delhi, Sasta Sahitya Mandal, 1953, pp. 58-68.
67. V.D. Majahan, *op. cit*, pp. 573-4.
68. Jayaprakash Narayan, *op.cit.*, p. 33.
69. *Ibid.*, p. 34.
70. *Ibid.*, p. 34.
71. *Ibid.*, p. 21.
72. V.D. Majahan, *op.cit.*, p. 574.
73. Anil Dutta Mishra, *op. cit.* p. 17.

5

Mahatma Gandhi and Sarvodaya

D. K. Oza

The word "Sarvodaya" is used so very often that atleast the young people do not know how the world was coined, its meaning, its history, its future.

Mahatma Gandhi, even when he was just a young lawyer, was a very careful reader of good books. He spent 22 years in South Africa and returned to India when he was 46 year old. Those were his most formative years (Remember he was born in 1869). When I was in South Africa along with a delegation of Indian Gandhians in 1991, our purpose was to see whether the two Institutions which Mahatma Gandhi founded in that country could be revived. Both Institutions go back to 100 years or more. One is called the Tolstoy Farm on the outskirts of Johannesburg and the other is called Phoenix Ashram on the outskirts of Durban. We had gone there on behalf of the Indian Council of Cultural Relations which is an organization created by the Government of India. Once during our 10-day visit there, we three members of the delegation were invited for lunch at a University. The Professor there told us "both Satyagraha and Sarvodaya were produced in South Africa and imported into India". I think this is a very accurate statement and we were amazed that a white South African (himself a staunched Gandhian) could make this very perceptive remark.

Mahatma Gandhi was very receptive to new ideas. Four persons profoundly influenced him—John Ruskin of England, Count Leo Tolstoy of Czarist Russia, Henry Thoreau of America and Srimad Raj Chandra of India. Look at young Gandhi's receptivity, openness and complete freedom from cultural prejudices! All four belong to four different nations. Of these, so far as Thoreau is concerned, young Gandhi read only his short essay "Civil Disobedience", but does not seem to have read his other classic "Walden". Even here, Thoreau's principle that "a bad law must be disobeyed" was one which Gandhi had already practiced in South Africa. His reading of the Essay by Thoreau merely gave him a much needed moral validation. The book by Tolstoy which influenced him is *The kingdom of God is Within You* and Gandhi did enter into a very short correspondence with that great Rishi of Russia. Srimad Raj Chandra, a devout Jain and scholar influenced Gandhi by his personal example—*Live in the World, but Live Detached.*

It is the fourth, John Ruskin, the Englishman whose book "Unto this Last" transformed Gandhi. The title of the book was borrowed by John Ruskin from *The Bible*. It is really a Biblical story. It goes like this—a man who was a big landholder wanted one-day a large number of labourers for helping in the harvest. His personal servant went into the market and hired quite a few labourers. But some came right at the beginning of the day, some two hours later, some four hours later and some six hours later. At the end of the day, the landholder paid the same wages to all of them. His personal servant was amazed and said "Master, why are you paying the same wages to those who came later and to those who came very early." The Master replied, "I must be fair Unto This Last." Philanthropy, charity, justice, love MUST reach the last person—the poor, the humiliated, the outcaste, the insulted, the powerless—must all be treated as equal. It was this teaching of Ruskin's book which hit Gandhi hard. He read the book during his overnight rail journey. He had the unchanging habit of practicing in his life whatever appealed to him. From the next day, he changed his life. In his 'Autobiography' he has given a very detailed description of the book and what he learnt from it.

This is it. Every human being is just that—a human being. Man or Woman or Child, the language, the culture, the nation, the education—nothing can diminish a human being. No distinctions, no discremination, no rejection, the affirmation of the humanity of everyone—glorious, unceasing, undiluted and unbiased. That is Sarvodaya. No claims to superiority, and no assertion of inferiority. That is Sarvodaya. All of us are children of the same God. All of us are parts of some divine principle. Do not trample upon anyone.

Help everyone, honour everyone, protect everyone. Unity and amity–no hatred, denunciation—That is Sarvodaya.

Essentially Sarvodaya includes a life of simplicity, truth, non-violence and the eleven vows which are on the first page of the book of *bhajans* which Gandhi personally supervised in preparation. This link between Sarvodaya and individual human virtues must be clearly understood.

I will conclude this by quoting Gandhi's own classic words—The Seven Sins are—Politics without principle; Wealth without work; Pleasure without conscience; Knowledge without character; Commerce without morality; Science without humanity and Worship without sacrifice.

6

Mahatma Gandhi and Non-Violence

S.N. Sahu

Today (September 23, 2005) early in the morning I stared reading Gandhi's writings from the Collected Works, Volume 71. The writings and speeches of Mahatma in that volume belonged to the period between 1930 and 1940 when the globe was gripped by the terrible Second World War and the consequences of which deeply agonised mankind. It was indeed ironic that the British rulers dragged India, the land of non-violence and the birthplace of Mahavir, Gautam Buddha and Mahatma Gandhi, to join the Second World War solely on the ground that they were ruling this country. It was indeed paradoxical that the world was seized by violence at a time when Gandhi's non-violence was so resoundingly successful in addressing some of the pressing and complex problems of humanity. Possibly the rulers at the time, particularly those horn Europe, were too blinded by l:1~eir preoccupation to conquer more territories and appropriate manifold resources to keep 'running their bourgeoning empires and satisfying their newly created synthetic desires.

Gandhi was very clear that the so-called democratic countries of Europe who are in the forefront of the battle against fascism are revised versions of the same doctrine against which they were fighting. It is interesting to note that he described the allied powers as the modified forms of tie axis powers. He appealed to the people of Poland, Czechoslovakia and the Jews of Germany and concluded that they could successfully defeat the violence of Hitler by following the path of unadulterated non-violence. His article "If I were a Czech", was one of the brilliant pieces articulating his ideas to non-violently confront the brutality and violence-inflicted that country. His appeal to the Jews that in the face of the mighty force of non-violence violence would melt was ridiculed by many in the world and even he was told that if a Gandhi emerged in Germany he would not survive even for five minutes, for he would be guillotined or taken to the concentration camp and put to death. His highly unconventional argument that non-violence might not succeed in one's lifetime and through sacrifice and suffering only one could patiently toil to see the triumph of non-violence failed to make any impact on the hardened sensibilities of the European rulers and war-stricken and war-weary peoples of Europe.

In spite of the non-acceptance and downright rejection of his ideas Gandhi never wavered from the path of non-violence. There are some critics who say that the Gandhi's non-violence would not have survived in any empire other than the British Empire. They advance the argument that the British Empire or the British rule was more benign than the rule of the Portuguese, Dutch, Japanese, French and other colonial rulers of that time. The reference to the so-called civilized rule of the British authorities and their attempts to introduce constitutional and liberal values as important factors behind the success of Gandhi as the foremost non-violent leader of mankind seems to be utterly false. Mahatma Gandhi while answering some questions of Frank Moraes wrote in 1941: "I assert that in India we have Hitlerian rule however disguised it may be in other terms." He dealt with the Hitlerian rule in India through non-violence.

Gandhi's concept of non-violence was the non-violence of the brave. The way the people of India and other leaders of India adopted the concept of non-violence indicated, in the words of Mahatma Gandhi, the non-violence of the weak. The question that comes to mind is that how Gandhi could integrate the principle of non-violence into his personality and how he could shape the consciousness of generations of people to follow the path of non-violence.

ONE has to remember that non-violence which Gandhi followed was no ordinary idea or belief. It was born of conviction and was based on the purification of the body and mind. It evolved through the control of the palate, non-possession of property or any other material or non-material thing, restraining one's senses, adoption of the principle of non-stealing, abolition of untouchability, promotion of communal harmony and, above all, anchoring life on moral principles and higher ideals. Non-violence thus did not mean only the nonuse of force, it was deeper in connotation and practice. It involved changing the whole way of life and consciousness and remaining in communion with nature and feeling that everything in this world is throbbing with the divine spirit of which the individual' is one small part. This identification of the individual with the whole cosmos and at the same time retaining the individuality constituted the core meaning of non-violence. Such a consciousness would obviously make one realise his or her shortcomings and propel him or her to constantly strive to refine his/her thought, action and behaviour.

A non-violent person of this type will be imbued with the true meaning of religion and not follow the ritualistic and established patterns of religious practices. Gandhi showed in his me that he was deeply religious and spiritual even as he hardly went to any temple or followed any dogma. He spearheaded many movements against British rule but never ever consulted any astrologer to decide the auspicious time to commence them. He never ever sought the blessings of the monks and sages who comfortably perched themselves in the monasteries of the Himalayas and pursued spiritual life completely oblivious of the social and economic degradation of people under the British rule. He had said that the concepts of truth and non-violence must come out of the cloistered surroundings, or the caves and monasteries and find application in the harsh realities of life. His assertion that spiritual regeneration—must include promotion education and improvement of social and economic standards and removal or all hindrances that come in the way of human progress amply spoke of the wider meaning of spiritualism which obviously could not be seen apart from life. Such a man, with full emphasis on self-control, spiritual development and the refinement of inner self, proclaimed that non-violence is a universal law and holds good in all times and climes.

Even Hitler's Germany could not have suppressed a personality whose extraordinary simplicity and profound spirituality was the source of non-violence. In fact, in 1940, in an appeal to the 'Europeans; Gandhi wrote that even if Hitler. Mussolini and Churchill come together they could not defeat what he has started in

India in a non-violent way. Europe had all the means to deal with violence but had no means to deal with non-violence. That is why non-violence evoked in him the deeper meaning of cosmic identity, curtailment of desires and keeping them in harmony with the essential necessities of life. A man who is so pure in thought, word and deed would be an amazing exponent and practitioner of non-violence. Gandhi was such a man and could have been so in any part of the world. Irrespective of the nature of regime and degree of brutality heaped on him.

In fact, he expressed his desire to die without harbouring ill will against his adversaries even if they resorted to unspeakable violence against him. His words written in. 1940 truly spoke of his innermost thoughts to remain non-violent amidst the brutalities of his assailants. He wrote:

> My non-violence will be tested and proved when r die peacefully under an assassin's axe. I should die like that, that is my cherished dream-on one side an axe is raised to strike me down, on the ether a dagger is pointed at me, a third person is wielding a club and a fourth is kicking and boxing me, r am standing peacefully in their midst asking people to remain peaceful and r die with a smile on my lips-I pray for such good fortune. I wish I could get this opportunity...

Eight years after he prophesied his death he came on the way of three bullets of hatred and stood firm with a stout heart uttering the name of Lord Ram. A few months before his martyrdom he wrote: "It would be enough for me if can die with truth and non-violence in my heart and Ram on my lips." A man imbued with such vision and wishing to suffer and face any—consequences could have been successful in defeating violence in any other country. The world is poorer without a Mahatma Gandhi and is yearning for such a noble soul.

7

Non-Violent Social Order: The Gandhian Way

G.V.V.S.D.S. Prasad

Societal progress depends upon the attitudes of people that constitute it. It is a constant endeavour to have these attitudes positive so that social life is possible. It would be a different thing when there is only one person living on this earth and hence he has no social obligations or responsibilities. If there is another person on this earth along with that person, what should be his behaviour, relationship and attitude towards that another? How should be treat, work, respect that another person? What should be his limits? And many such questions arise where there are two or more persons in a society.

The essence of societal relations is Truth and Non-violence. One should be truthful to another. Truth is the basis or foundation for all human relations. Truth follows that these relations should be based on Non-violence. That ensures peace and love. Peace is not merely the absence of tensions but presence of justice. Peace gives us happiness which is an object of all pursuits. Loving other people, beings is an essential element in society. We have to see ourselves in others. We should treat others as we want them to treat us. We respect them as we expect ourselves to be respected. This mutuality is necessary for a cohesive society. The peace should start with oneself. I should be at peace with myself. This inner peace should extend to family, community, society, nation and the whole world. Individual should be the origin of building a peaceful society.

To be peaceful, to radiate love one should be non-violent. We are living in a society which is experiencing escalating violence.

People are becoming impatient, angry and restive. They do not know what their anxiety is for. They seem to be perpetually hungry. Non-violence is a way of life. It is an attitude and state of mind. We at the individual level should cultivate nonviolence in thought, word and deed. We should refuse to allow an offensive thought, anger or ill will against anyone else. In fact, we know that anger affects our body metabolism. It can lead to several disorders and harms the author himself. We should also cultivate the habit of using a non-offensive language in our talks and writings. It should not hurt others or raise negative passions in others. Similarly our actions also should not be violent. The practice of non-violence at the individual level is the foundation for non-violence in society. It is the violence in individual life that supports violence in society.

The violence in society is manifest in several forms. We experience the growing violence and its harmful effects everyday. It is not only increase in violence but the increase in its intensity, methods, tools and the cruel attitudes. Why should there be so much of hatred that supports a violent pattern of society? We see an increase in crime rate. From crime related to property, we see vandalism, killings, violence against women, children etc. We are also experiencing the problem of extremist violence that stems from the belief that societal change is possible only through violence. We see bombing of trains or public places killing innocent people. There is a growing uncertainty if we can return home safe. There is no relationship, hatred or any other problem between the perpetrator of the crime and the victims who die or get wounded. It is a sheer cruelty and a mind of devilish passion. Violence results in counter violence too. The retaliatory violence that the State resorts to or the one intended to curb the extremist violence too takes its toll. Citizen get sandwiched between violence of both the sides. Many a political agitations resort to violence. It is believed as a form to get attention as non-violent protests do not draw the attention of policy makers.

The other form of violence is war. Countries all over the world acquired such combat capabilities with weapons of mass destruction that can spell the doom's day. The nuclear weapons, hydrogen bomb, biological weapons, chemical weapons have such destructive potential that the life on the planet can be wiped out more than 100 times. Should we appreciate the advancements in science and technology that man has achieved or feel sad about the self-destructive tendencies of man? The choice before the mankind is non-violence or non-existence.

In addition to these direct forms of violence, the indirect forms are more far reaching. Its damage and toll is much more than the direct–incident related violence that would leave some dead. Possibly, the indirect forms of violence supports the direct forms of violence. Poverty is a form of violence. Is there any person in this world who wishes to remain poor by choice? No. But the fact remains that a majority of population of the world reel under object poverty. Why? Is it that some have a vested interest in perpetuating this poverty? Is their poverty linked to the prosperity of some others?

Ignorance and illiteracy are another form of violence.

Child labour is a form of violence. Children who should be in the school enjoying their childhood are forced to earn and support their families. Will they not grow and develop with animosity against the society that had robbed them of their childhood? Will it not lead to hatred and resultant crime?

Discrimination is another form of violence. All humans are equal. Why should some be treated as high and others as low by birth? If the high or low of one's respectability should depend, it should be on what their contribution to the society had been and not on where they were born. Untouchability, casteism, regionalism, linguistic chauvinism, communal passions are all forms of violence.

You go to a government office for a work of a public nature and a bribe is demanded of you. Will you not be annoyed? Corruption is another form of violence. It has now grown in size and acceptance that is considered necessary for smooth functioning of public affairs.

You also encounter enormous pollution on the streets. We have a right to pollution free environment. But our air, water, land are all polluted. Depletion of ozone layer, global warming are threatening the mankind and all this is violence against the mother earth and humanity at large.

Violence in individual lives and the indirect forms of violence together support the direct forms of violence. For all these forms of violence what is the root cause? How are our attitudes responsible for these happenings?

Our society had value foundations based on truth, non-violence, contentment, humility, respect for nature, live and let live, etc. Now these values give place to greed, desire for unlimited accumulation. What was a cohesive community once is now destroyed and is reduced to a crowd. Mutual dependence, respect and togetherness do not allow exploitative relations. When this personal touch is gone, mutual obligations disappear, human values are gone, anyone can become an object for exploitation. This greed leads to manipulations, untruthfulness, fraud, corruption, segregation, denial, hatred, violence and war. All these follow as an inevitable outcome of greed.

The essence is whether we are contended with what we have or what is 'ours'. If we cross the line and aspire for some thing which is not ours we give up all values or create arguments to interpret that, that something is mine. We allow the ascendancy of expressions, "Might is Right", "Survival of the Fittest", "Money makes many things" and the like. We realize that people wish to acquire wealth as fast as possible exploiting others or destroying the nature.

The society has gone into subtle forms of exploitation from the direct forms like Extortion (theft, robbery, corruption, cheating etc.), Slavery, Feudalism (bonded labour), Imperialism (political domination for economic exploitation) to a market operated exploitation. Purchasing decisions are influenced by attractive advertisements. We should be wary of these designs and protect ourselves against these tendencies. Violence in any form is going to leave behind its evil results. Hence the need for a non-violent society that ensures peace with justice.

> Love is creative and redemptive. Love builds-up and unites; hate tears down and destroys. The aftermath of the 'fight with fire' method which you suggest is bitterness and chaos, the aftermath of the love method is reconciliation and creation of the beloved community. Physical force can repress, restrain, coerce, destroy,

but it cannot create and organize anything permanent; only love can do that. Yes, love—which means understanding, creative, redemptive goodwill, even for one's enemies—is the solution to the race problem.

—***Martin Luther King, Jr.***

8

Non-Violence: The New Culture of Revolution

Lavanam

September 11, 1906 Johannesburg (South Africa) Empire Theatre: It was packed from floor to ceiling with about 3,000 Indians. Men, Women and Children; from North and South; Hindus, Muslims and Christians; from Telugus, Tamilians to Gujaratis and Punjabis. After Mohandas Karamchand Gandhi spoke to them, they took a pledge in one voice that they would offer Satyagraha against the injustices perpetuated against Indians by the South African Government. Thus Satyagraha was born 100 years ago. It was the dawn of a new culture of revolution. Till then the culture of revolution was violence. Now the new culture of revolution was non-violence and civility. Gandhi was the first person to think on these lines and put into practice.

Though Satyagraha was born in 1906, the foundation for it was laid in May 1893, just a week after 24-year-old Gandhi landed in South Africa at Durban. When he started the journey from Durban to Pretoria, his destination, at Maritzburg Railway Station he was kicked out of the first class compartment. As in those days the practice was that free Indians could travel by first class as long as there was no White passenger. From Durban to Martizburg there was no White passenger, and also Gandhi did not know about this practice. So, at Martizburg when a White passenger entered the compartment, Gandhi did not get down. This furiated the White man. There was an argument, which resulted in a scuffle that ended in violently throwing Gandhi out of the first class compartment on to the platform. That incident made Gandhi think about self-respect of the human being. This consciousness about the human self-respect was unable to accept the violence suffered by Gandhi. Gandhi did not want to pay back in the same coin. He pondered over. Soon his thoughts matured to search for a new culture of revolution. Till then every revolution, every struggle, every response to indignities and injustices resulted only in violence. Gandhi said violence supported untruth and inequalities. So if he reached through violence to any injustice, he would be cementing the continuity of violence with a feeling of revenge and to destroy the opponent. Gandhi felt eye for eye and eye for eye would result in continuance of eye for eye, which would make the whole world blind. Gandhi's this feeling was excellently described by Louis Fisher. *You cannot inject new ideas into a man's head by chopping it off; neither will you infuse a new spirit into his heart by piercing it with dagger.* Not only that, violence increases cruelty in the practitioner and the attitude of hitting back with revenge in the sufferer. This situation breeds continuous animosity. Gandhi wanted reason and compassion to guide the both. That was what achieved on September 11, 1906. That small achievement led the humanity on a new path, the path of non-violence.

Non-violence is not just absence of violence. It is a positive way of life based on truth and love. Satyagraha means insistence on truth. Truth is that all people are equal and they should live equal in social respect, economic opportunity and political power. This non-violent struggle produced wonderful results in South Africa where the weapon was not outside the warrior's body. It is neither sword nor gun. It is self-respect and self-confidence of every individual to treat every other individual with mutual respect and mutual trust. This is the birth of new human in a new civilization. That was what started 100 years.

Ever since, violence has come to its logical conclusion in producing and using the Atom Bomb. Now the choice is not between violence and non-violence. But the choice is between non-existence and non-violence. Today we are suffering from both, concealed violence i.e. exploitation and open violence which is leading to total annihilation. In this situation Freedom and Self-respect of individuals are challenged everywhere. As human values are diminishing people are getting divided only as exploiters and exploited the suppressors and the suppressed. Non-violence tries to educate both to think of self-respect and mutual respect. It wants to liberate both the suppressed and suppressors from the cobweb of helplessness. Helplessness creates slaves and tyrants. Non-violence liberates people both from slave mind and tyranny. Then both become strong and equal with self-respect and mutual respect.

Thus Gandhi's Satyagraha creates a new human and a new civilization. Both in South Africa and in the freedom struggle of India under the leadership of Gandhi thousands and millions of people practised this and achieved considerably. After Gandhi Martin Luther King, Lech Walesa, Dalai Lama, Desmond Tutu, Nelson Mandela, Aung San Suu Kyi and others continued this new culture of revolution. It is not easy to change the old ways. Hence, though, their achievements are spectacular, still, humanity has to go a long way in brightening the light of this new culture to throw away the darkness of violence, exploitation and suppression. It is our responsibility to go forward.

9

Globalization: Concept and Nature

Anil Dutta Mishra

The real wealth of a nation is its people. And the purpose of development is to create an enabling environment for people to enjoy long, healthy and creative lives. This simple but powerful truth is too often forgotten in the pursuit of material and financial wealth.

– Human Development Report, 1990

Introduction

Globalization is not new but the present era has some distinctive features such as shrinking space, shrinking time and disappearing borders are linking people's lives more deeply, more intensively and more immediately than ever before. Globalization is a process integrating not just the economy but culture, technology and governance. Globalization is considered to be neo-liberal. Its normative base is the celebration of the market. In other words, it is a triumph – not only over so- called global "historic alternatives" [F. Fukuyama (92). The End of History and the Last Man] but also over unions and Keynesian states. In fact, elites on behalf of the states are real authors of globalization.

Globalization has become the current Mantra or even panacea to solve all human problems. It is believed that the achievements of globalization would make the people all over globe happy, prosperous and contended and that there would be no conflicts, no poverty and inequality, no violation of human rights, no malnutrition, no illiteracy, and no disease, etc. Each individual and community would be so integrated with the world that the benefits would flow both laterally and vertically so smoothly that no one would remain untouched by prosperity. There would be nation state without boundary. It is said that global markets, global technologies, global ideas and global solidarity can enrich the lives of people everywhere, greatly expanding their choices. The growing interdependence of people's lives calls for shared values and a shared commitment to the human development of all people. This era of globalization is opening many opportunities for millions of people around the world. Increased trade, new technologies, foreign investments, expanding media and Internet connections are fuelling economic growth and human advance. All these offer enormous potential eradicate poverty in the 21st century. Today we have more wealth and technology—and more commitment to a global community—than ever before.

But reality is totally different. Recently there has been increasing disillusionment among policy-makers in several parts of the world and some fundamental questions are asked. These are: Who want globalization? Globalization for what and for whom? Why is globalization of human resource not taking place? Do people want globalization? It is said that the issue of globalization is receiving considerable attention but no work is being done on the social costs involved (in terms of poverty, inequality, unemployment and tensions) nor on the growing marginalization of people in India as well as in other developing countries. The progress in areas like health, education and other social sectors are slowed by the diversion of precious human resources for national security and in combating terrorism and separatist movement. It is also said that the culture of consumerism is the product of globalization. Almost all the consumer items that are being promoted to sustain the economic growth have significant impact on nation and society directly or indirectly. The concept of globalization and the culture of consumerism are antithetical for all that Indian culture stands for. The new information technology and advances in telecommunications have tended to erode the heterogeneity of national life styles, social and economic values and even cultures. This is visible in the standardization of consumer tastes in favour of fast foods (evidenced by the omnipresence of Mc Donald's and Coca Cola) and American films and soap operas. Consumerism is based on domination, hegemony, exploitation, alienation, concentration of knowledge, wealth and power. On the Few top TNCs of the developed nations have increased their profits manifold, on the one hand, a very significant majority of people around the world are still struggling for their basic needs and existence. The people of Asia, Africa and Latin American regions are still not part of the globalization.

In the present scenario, globalization is irreversible and unstoppable. Most of the countries of the world, willingly or unwillingly, have already accepted it and others may have to accept it. However, it is mostly agreed that globalization should be introduced with human face for the benefit of the poor and needy. The challenges arising out of globalization require total newness on all fronts—from government to NGOs levels. In this article an attempt has been made to analyse the broad concept of globalization and its effects on people in terms of growth and productivity, poverty and income distribution, as well as employment.

Globalization: A Conceptual Analysis

Globalization means different things to different people according to their ideology and perception. The word globalization is used in two ways. In a positive sense, it is used to describe a process of increasing integration into the world economy. In other words, it means the expansion of economic activities across national boundaries. It is also used to prescribe a strategy of development based on a rapid integration with the world economy and view it as salvation. In other words, globalization is a process associated with increasing economic openness, growing economic interdependence and deepening economic integration in the global economy. In negative sense, it is seen as domination by developed nations over developing nations. In most of the countries, particularly those belonging to the developing world, liberalization policy has not been evolved indigenously. It has been adopted under World Bank—IMF combine conditionality of which internal and external liberalization policies are integral part.

Globalization is not new. Recall the early sixteenth century and the late nineteenth. But this era is different:

> *New Markets*—foreign exchange and capital markets are linked globally, operating 24 hours a day, with dealings at a distance in real time.

New Tools—Internet links, cellular phones, media networks.

New Actors—The World Trade Organization (WTO) with authority over national governments, the multinational corporations with more economic power than many states, the global networks of Non-Governmental Organizations (NGOs) and other groups that transcend national boundaries.

New Rules—multilateral agreements on trade, services and intellectual property, backed by strong enforcement mechanisms and more binding for national governments, reducing the scope for national policy.

According to the World Development Report (2000 - 01) five actions are necessary:

- Promoting global financial stability and opening the markets of rich countries to the agricultural goods, manufactures and services of poor countries.
- Bridging the digital and knowledge divides, thus bringing technology and information to people throughout the world.
- Providing financial and non-financial resources for international public goods especially medical and agricultural research.
- Increasing aid and debt relief to help countries to take actions to end poverty within a comprehensive framework.
- Giving a voice to poor countries and poor people in global forums.

The key features of globalization are: *(a)* Economic features: Growth in Trade; Growth in FDI and Capital Flows; Global Production and consumption; Global competition; Trade and Investment Liberalization Policies *(b)* Non- Economic Features: Loss of National Sovereignty; Standardization of values and cultures. In other word, a major feature of globalization is the growing concentration and monopolization of economic resources and power by transnational corporations and by global financing firms and funds and globalization of national policies and policy-making mechanisms. National policies (including in economic, social, cultural and technological areas) that until recently were under the jurisdiction of States and people within a country have increasingly come under the influence of international agencies and processes or of big private corporations and economic/ financial players. This led to erosion of national sovereignty and narrowed the ability of governments and people to make choices from options in economic, social and cultural policies. Governments now have to implement policies that are in line with the decisions and rules of these international institutions. The key institutions concerned are the World Bank, the International Monetary Fund (IMF) and the WTO.

The other fundamental premise of globalization is the relatively unhindered flow of goods and capital (but not people) across national boundaries. There are three economic manifestations of this phenomenon—international trade, international investment and international finance. Globalization requires country's openness to the world economy. There are four elements that are conventionally considered in determining a country's openness to the world economy. There is, most importantly, *(i)* the proportion of a country's Gross Domestic Product (GDP) that is involved in the international trade of goods and services. Than there is *(ii)* the related element of the level of tariffs, which speaks to the degree of protection accorded to local production against imports from the world economy. Beyond trade there is *(iii)* the element of the degree of transnationalisation of production, that is, the extent to which exchange of capital takes place for purposes of production; for the less developed countries, it refers primarily to the import of Foreign Direct Investment (FDI). Transnationalisation of production stands on a different footing from international trade, even though trade is involved prior or subsequent to the production process. Essentially, while in the area of international trade during the era of globalization the relevant actors treat the world as a global market, in the internationalization of production the relevant actors treat the world as a global factory, the different constituent parts or division of which are located in several countries, yet from a single production system. Finally, but not unrelated to the previous elements, in *(iv)* the extent of state controls on capital movements

It is very common to hear the words privatization, globalization and liberalization. In fact, privatization and globalization are inherent in liberlization. The theoretical foundations for the policy of liberalization including privatization are provided by several interrelated strands of literature mainly contributed by New Right

Schools of Thought, Property Rights Literature, the Principal – agent Relationship and Organization and Management Literature. In all there are four New Right Schools of Thought. These are *(i)* the Chicago School led by Friedman; *(ii)* the Austrian School led by Hayek; *(iii)* Public Choice School led by Buchanan, Tullock and Niskanen; and *(iv)* the supply side Economics School led by Laffer, Gilder and Wanniski. The New Right Schools of thought, in spite of intellectual differences, broadly maintain that state involvement leads to increasing monopoly, increasing budget and suppressing of entrepreneurial behaviour, limiting choice, over production of unwanted services and encouragement to waste and inefficiency. In view of this the New Right has forcefully argued retrieval of the State as a regulator and producer. Therefore, deregulation/ liberalization and privatization are amongst six-point reform agenda of the New Right. The other measures are the reduction of inflation, lower taxation, increasing role of market forces in the provision of public services and institutional and constitutional reforms. The aim of these reforms is to promote competition between rival bureaucracies, reduce the influence of interest groups and corporatist institutions and impose a constitutional upper limit on the public expenditure as a proportion of the gross national product.

The theoretical base of globalization is directly rooted in the principle of comparative advantage, specialization in the production of goods and services based on factor endowment and competition results in benefits to all countries in international trade. In the open economy model (i.e. economy having linkages with global market), international trade leads to factor price equalization and optimum pattern of resource allocation globally.

Globalization is a calculated imperialist design of hegemonization in economic, political, ecological and cultural terrains, threatening loss of economic, self-reliance and political sovereignty, erosion of democratic structures and damaging of plural cultural identities. Not only this, employment of protectionist policies, discriminatory trade-conditions, direct intervention in the domestic affairs of LDCs regarding their intellectual property right amount to virtual 'trade war' and destabilization of the fragile economies and strife-ridden politics of the latter. Globalism would remain an idle fancy in the absence of genuine 'inter-nationalism' that is, egalitarian interaction among nations.

As a culmination of the unbridled, unrestrained 'multi-national' capitals, globalization leaves the poorer counties behind in global competition, as the clear objective of capital mobility is profit, prestige and power for its owners and not the well-being of the people at large. This is confirmed by historical and empirical evidence. It is intrinsic to the nature of capital, as articulated by Lenin most vociferously, to more towards exploitable resources. As investments capital has moved and modernized, it has also in the process exploited people and natural resources and often left behind pollution, poverty, inequality, injustice, crime, corrupting and a general degradation of environment—a record not much different from the imperialist history of aggressive capitalism, obsessed with growth.

Globalization is a totalizing process interims of both hegemonization and homogenization, and extended and subtler American version of European colonial/imperialist ambitions of domination, expropriating and transforming the world in its own image. Ideologically also, it is a derivative of the earlier conceptualizations of 'progress' and 'modernization', premised on the West-centric view of civilization, materialism and economies glorification of the 'invisible hand' of the market, growth—observed industrial industrialism, objectification of nature and an instrumental treatment of humanity.

The specter of mass resistance and political movements is on the anvil in a majority of third world societies that have set out in the direction of globalization, constantly haunting and scaring to generate chaos and degeneration of whatever little is achieved by these societies. It appears that eventually globalization will prove to be a disaster for the developing societies that will push them into the oblivion of anarchy and instability reminiscent of the Hobbesean state of nature.

The Reality of Globalization

The end of 20th century witnessed ushering in of an epoch of new world order in which the idea of globalization found expression and flourished under the auspices and blessings of Breton Wood institutions—notably the World Bank and International Monetary Fund—paving a way for the neo-capitalist hegemony and subjugation in a more vigorous but civilized manner. As a matter of fact globalization is a latest dream selling exercise on the part of U.S.

promising a transparent, free and rational world order, which will ultimately culminate into an ideal Global Village.

Liberalization, privatization and globalization are the buzzwords in contemporary world. All goals end here. Privatization worldwide began in 1980's because of rising debt and low commodity prices. Eastern Europe, Russia, Ukraine, Argentina, Brazil, Hungry, Mexico, Poland have already gone through the process. In support of privatization it is said that direct state involvement in commercial activities conflicts with its other roles. The real picture of liberalization, privatization and globalization is quite different and complex.

Uruguay Round agreement brought the WTO into existence. WTO agreements' appears to be based on the hypothesis that liberalization is the panacea for all ills in the economy, trade and commerce for the society The Uruguay Round agreement not only reduced trade barriers — by an average of 40 per cent — but also laid down rules for what kinds of policies governments can make on matters such as intellectual property and investment, making its impact more complex, more expensive to employment and more difficult to predict. It is generally advocated that the free trade would lead to higher rates of economic growth. But the fact is that economic globalization and trade liberalization have concentrated power in the larger entities we know as transnational corporations. It is the TNCs which have benefitted the most in the era of globalization. Small farmers are unable to compete in the global economy and are being driven off their land, leaving the door wide open to the corporations. Free trade has enslaved the hungry rather than freed them. Trade can help to achieve food security, but only if it is democratic and free from corporate control; only if it helps rather than hinders the poor. Further, about one-third of the global trade conducted by the MNCs is instrumental in liquidating national economies. In the political sphere, the nation— states find themselves increasingly constrained, as new enters of power emerge to delimit political sovereignty in terms of foreign aid, IMF loans, deregulation, etc. Growing concentration of economic 'resources and political power has also aggravated social schisms and conflicts.

The modern world has corporate – managed trade rather than free trade. The trade liberalization has failed the poor and stands in danger of giving trade as a whole a bad name. The poor are going hungry because of the way the trading system is working. Trade liberalization—'free' trade, trade without barriers—is harming, not helping them. The trade liberalization that the WTO oversees appears to be failing the poor, hindering rather than helping them, and handing power to transnational corporations.

India urged that developing countries be allowed greater autonomy in establishing and supporting domestic agricultural policy. A purely market-based approach might not be appropriate for developing countries, it said; for some countries, it might be necessary to adopt a market- plus approach, in which non-trade concerns such as the maintenance of the livelihoods of the agrarian peasantry and the production of sufficient food to meet domestic needs are taken into consideration... [W]hile it may not be possible to immediately ensure that developing countries are able to produce at least a minimum percentage of their annual food requirements, this is a goal that has to be pursued.

Globalization has an adverse effect on poor developing countries with an inadequate national capacity. Almost all the countries of the Third World have signed the WTO. While most have gained, the poorest, 800 million hungry people, have lost. Any society, national or international, will ultimately be judged on whether its systems, rules and regulations assist the most needy. By that criterion, the current international trade system is failing. People go hungry because they are too poor to grow enough or to buy enough food. On the other hand, in the late 1990s the world, as a whole, spent more than US $500 billion to combat the supposed 'millennium bug'—ten times more than rich countries give to the poor each year in development assistance. By contrast, the amount needed to have world hunger free by 2015—a target agreed at the 1996 World Food Summit—would be US $60 billion dollars over 15 years, or US $4 billion per year in increased spending, hardly an excessive amount.

Globalization is transforming trade, finance, employment, migration, technology, communications, entertainment, the environment, social systems, values, ways of living, patterns of thinking, cultures and patterns of governance. Unemployment, poverty, inequality and alienation are increasing, partly as a result of globalization. Crime, drugs, terrorism, violence, civil wars, diseases and environmental destruction are becoming globalized. Capital, technology and advanced skills dominate the more reality dispensable factors: unskilled labour and the environment. Cost reductions are carried out and labour and nature suffer. Globalization offers great opportunity for human advance — but only the stronger governance.

The globalization of production is weakening state-centric schemes for implementing economic, social and cultural rights, most dramatically in the wealthier countries of the Northern Hemisphere. It does not however seem to be creating viable alternative mechanisms. Semi-permanent unemployment, attributable in part to the development of increasingly global mechanisms of production and exchange, has already led to a modest shrinking of the welfare state in many countries in Western Europe.

In any case, the impact of globalization on economy, society and polity extends beyond external openness in respect of foreign trade, tariff levels, transnationalisation of production and capital controls. The existing attraction of globalization as well as international pressures, such as from the WTO, encourage domestic policy changes in an effort to bring about greater institutional convergence with the more advanced economies. These policy changes in turn, are likely to have additional impact on economy, society and polity.

Globalization is very uneven process, with unequal distribution of benefits and losses. This imbalance leads to polarization between the few countries and groups that gain, and the many countries and groups in society that lose out or are marginalized. Globalization, polarization, wealth concentration and marginalization are therefore linked through the same process. A World Bank study finds that the poorest 40 per cent of people in developing countries have seen their incomes fall since liberalization began. The evidence is powerful and it discredits the claims of Western government ministers that trade liberalization lessens poverty. The rapid growth of the global economy in recent decades is perhaps most clearly shown by the fact that in 1970 the total number of Transnational Corporations (TNCs) was about 700, but grew by 1998 to at least 53,607 TNCs that were contracted with at least 448,917 foreign subsidiaries. The six largest corporations in the world (Exxon, General Motors, Ford, Mitsu, Daimler- Chrysler, and Mitsubishi) have combined revenues larger than the combined budgets of 64 nations that include 58 percent of the world's population (including India, Indonesia, Brazil,

Russia, Pakistan, Bangladesh, Nigeria and Mexico). Only seven nations have budgets larger than Ford, Exxon or General Motors: namely France, the United Kingdom, Italy, China, Japan, Germany, and the United States. Size of individual corporations in comparison to nations is impressive. However, their growing influence based on their growing number makes them even more powerful.

The world has become more polarized, with the gulf between the poor and rich of the world widening in recent years. From 1970 to 2000, the share of the poorest 20 per cent rose from 70 per cent to 85 per cent. Uneven globalization is bringing not only integration but also fragmentation, dividing communities and nations. In the aftermath of liberalization, manufacturing by license has given way to competitive manufacturing. Free trade is merely the global manifestation of the division of labour. The forces of global integration and technological advance can and must be harnessed to serve the interests of poor people. In 2000, of the world 6 billion people, 2.8 billion live on less than $2 a day and 1.2 billion on less than $1 a day. Six infants of every 100 do not see their first birthday, and 8 do not survive to their fifth. Of those who do reach school age, 9 boys in 100 and 14 girls do not go to primary school. These conceal extra ordinary diversity and variations.

Globalization has divided the world into several factions that may be called Davos, Seatlle, Moscow, Beijing, Tehran and Okinawa factions. The Davos faction includes some 1000 state and corporate elites that annually meet at Davos, Switzerland, to chart the course of globalization. It represents the interests of the Global 1000 largest TNCs and OECD group of rich nations. The Seatle Faction consists of those in the advanced capitalist countries protesting against World Trade Organization in Seatle last year, because their lives have been dislocated by globalization. The Moscow Faction is composed of those countries that by reason of their own failures or discrimination are being left out of the globalization bandwagon. The Beijing faction consists of those countries that have more or less successfully jumped on the bandwagon in the hope of benefiting from its fruits. As a Crossroad of Japanese, Chinese, Southeast Asian, and Western civilizations, the Tehran Faction could be interpreted to include the Islamic militant movement protesting against the economic, political and cultural domination of a western world order. The most eloquent spokesperson for its views happens to be but a secular Christian Palestinian nationalist, Edward said.

Globalization is thus affecting different categories of countries differently. This process can broadly be categorized as follows: growth and expansion in the few leading or fully participating countries; moderate and fluctuating growth in some countries attempting to fit into the globalization/liberalization framework; and marginalization or deterioration experienced by many countries unable to get out of acute problems such as low commodity prices and debt, unable to benefit from export opportunities. The UNCTAD report also warns of the risks, stating "the process of globalization and liberalization can also give rise to a number of potential negative consequences and challenges to development." It gives details of the following three problems: lose of policy autonomy (the range of policy instruments available to developing countries has narrowed as a result of economic liberalization policies and stringent multilateral disciplines); financial openness and the risk of sentiments of external investor; and the phenomenon of marginalization (in which some developing countries, specially LDCs, are unable to benefit from or meaningfully participate in globalization due to structural structural supply—side weakness and debt.)

The uneven and unequal nature of the present globalization process is manifested in the fast- growing gap between the world's rich and poor people and between developed and developing countries, and in the large differences among nations in the distribution of gains and losses.

A large number of people in the developed and developing nation have strong reservations about the benefits of globalization to the poor nations and they have shown their resentment through protests on various. In advance of Seattle meeting, more than 1,200 NGOs from nearly a hundred countries—from environmentalists to labour unions, Third World development groups to consumer organizations—signed a 'stop the WTO round' petition. The international trading system, said the petitioners, is inequitable, un-transparent and in conflict with national and international regimes that promote high environment and development standards. They proposed a fundamental review of the system, and the development of "an alternative, humane and sustainable international system of trade and investment relations." And they urged governments to "move away from the habit of shaping their international trade policies around offensive interests of large Transnational. Corporations." The recent meeting of WTO in France was also protested by the large number of people.

India and Liberalization

The aim of structural reform programme was to attain a higher rate of growth on sustainable basis through efficiency and productivity originating from relaxation of government controls over production, investment and prices in the domestic economy and progressively opening up of the Indian economy to foreign trade, capital and technology. The structural reform measures constitute the core of the economic liberalization.

Liberalization in India has two dimensions—internal and external.The domestic liberalization policy encompasses all facets of the Indian economy. However, thrust areas are industry, public enterprises, taxation, financial and infrastructure sectors.

The industrial sector has witnessed far-reaching reforms. The New Industrial Policy, 1991 abolished compulsory licensing for all except a few industries. The reform has enabled the taking out of the licensing system for more than 90 per cent of the industrial sector. In case of existing units all major expansions are exempted from licensing. The existing and new units are provided a new broad banding facility with a view to enabling them to produce any article without an additional investment.

In the area of public enterprises five major reforms have been introduced. First, monopoly of the state sector has been drastically reduced from seventeen to four. That is, thirteen industries have been opened to private sector, which was hitherto monopoly of the state sector. This is known as disguised privatization. Within existing public enterprises, sweeping changes favouring increasing role of market forces are in progress. These include performance improvement through a Memorandum of Understanding (MOU) system, referring of sick enterprises to the Board for Industrial and Financial Reconstruction (BIFR) for the formulation of revival/rehabilitation schemes or closure and enhanced autonomy to select public enterprises for enabling them to become global and domestic players.

Privatization has not been explicitly referred to in the NIP, 1991. Initially, the word privatization, it seems has been avoided partly due to political considerations. In the first budget (1991-92) immediately after the announcement of NIP, 1991, limited selling of government equity under the name of disinvestments policies was mentioned. The selling of government equity below 50 per cent continued till late nineties. It is during October 1999 budget that a full-fledged privatization policy was announced. Under privatization policy, 13 public enterprises and 21 hotels owned by the government have already been privatized.

Based on the recommendations of Chelliah Committee and Raikhi Committee tax reforms comprise of moderate rate of taxation, broadening the tax base, simplification in compliance and extension of Modified Value Added Tax (MODVAT) to other areas. Financial sector reforms consist of slashing of Statutory Liquidity Ratio (SLR) and thus increasing the availability of funds with banks, allowing private banks to expand, encouraging new entrants, simplification and rationalization of the interest rate structure. The Government has also opened insurance sector to private sector. The capital market is undergoing similar reforms.

The infrastructure sectors particularly telecommunication, power and roads which were traditionally monopolies have also been opened to the private sector.

External liberalization (i.e. globalization) in India has covered areas such as trade, foreign exchange, capital and technology. The major initiatives include current account convertibility of rupee, allowing exchange rate of rupee to be determined by the market forces in foreign exchange markets, abolition of import through licensing except for consumer goods, drastic reduction in import duties overtime, automatic approval of Reserve Bank of India for foreign equity in select high priority industries, the provision of automatic approval for technology agreements in select high priority industries. In addition Foreign Institutional Investors (FIIs) registered with RBI are permitted to operate in the capital market. Large number of incentives are provided to Non-Resident Indians (NRIs) and Overseas Corporate Bodies (OCB) to invest in India. Indians firms are also allowed to raise capital from International market through Global Depository Receipts (GDRs) and Foreign Currency Convertible Bonds (FCCBs).

Scarcity of income distribution data, obviously, makes it very difficult to arrive at precise assessment of the impact of Globalization on income inequalities, but it is clear that even after nearly one decade of advent of Globalization in India a vast gulf exists between the different income-earners with, as per World Development Report, 1999, top 20 per cent of the population accounting for 39.3 per cent of the total income while share of the bottom 20 per cent was only 9.2 per cent.

The point about retailing the foregoing data about persistence of individual-level poverty is that it gives rise to doubts about the positive pay-offs of Globalization as far as the regional inequalities also are concerned. While data sets about income inequalities at individual or percentile and decline levels are relatively scarce, a number of regional or inter-state inequalities data-sets have been generated making it possible to assess the impact of Globalization on a real disparities.

According to Economic Times Research, the annual data show that over the period 1996 to 2000, 38 per cent of the companies declared losses at the net level in 2000 as compared to 16 per cent in 1996. In the period of economic reforms does the loss making companies whose percentage has increased represent the cost of liberalization.

The cost of economic reforms is also reflected in the number of cases with the Board for Industrial and Financial Reconstruction (BIFR). BIFR till the year 1998 has compiled figures about sick companies on the edge of closure. A total net worth of Rs. 17,815.56 cr. has been wiped out two and half times over by accumulated losses amounting to Rs. 7,159.54 cr. Over 2,454 units across 19 industries are affecting around 15 lakh workers. The extent of human disaster is particularly acute in industries like textiles, metallurgy and jute etc.

The various Rounds of Surveys conducted by the National Sample Survey Organization (NSSO) revel that the average annual growth rate of overall employment (in both the organized and unorganized sectors) was 2.73 per cent annum in the period 1972-73 to 1977-78 but declined to 1.54 per cent per annum in 1983 to 1987-88 to 1993-94. As per the 55th Round (July 1999 – June 2000) of the Survey on employment conducted by the NSSO overall employment grew by about 1 per cent per annum during 1993-94 to 1999-2000. Employment in absolute numbers has risen from 303 million on 1983 to 374 million in 1994 (2.04%) and to 397 million in 2000 (0.98%). The labour force participation rate deceleration in the growth of the labour force from 2.29 per cent annum in 1987-88 to 1993-94, to 1.03 per cent per annum in the period 1993-94 to 1999-2000.

A more detailed scrutiny of the inter-state variations in the growth-pattern (UNDP, 1999) shows that two states with high per capita income in 1980-91 viz. Punjab and Haryana lost momentum in the nineties while Maharashtra and Gujarat overshot them indicating that during the Globalization era the Green Revolution lost steam while industry-based growth of Maharashtra and Gujarat was gathering speed. In case (and the probabilities of this being the case are high) economic momentum of Punjab and Haryana declines further the inequalities between the different states of the Indian federal system would certainly be aggravated significantly. In more specific terms, states like Tamil Nadu, Kerala, West Bengal, Madhya Pradesh, Andhra Pradesh and Karnataka would continue to stay at their current GNP ranks while Panjab and Haryana would decline and Guajarat and Maharashtra forge ahead while Uttar Pradesh, Bihar and Orissa would continue to remain at the bottom unless those associated with "public governance" address this issue of persisting areal imbalances directly rather than letting the markets (read: MNCs) adopt their basic policy of "Betting upon the strong."

Thus, a worrisome aspect of the impact of Globalization upon the state economies is revealed by the fact there are not only wide-ranging areal differentials in terms of decline of poverty in India but the "Green Revolution" states are finding it difficult to sustain their (low) poverty-shares. While Punjab and Haryana had, till recently taken giant strides in poverty reduction, but, Haryana has already begun to slip with its BPL share in population rising from 0.92 per cent in 1983-84 to 1.83 per cent in 1987-88 and then dipping but still remaining higher at 1.37 per cent in 1993-94 than 1983-84. More recent Planning Commission data updated to 1999-2000 has shown that Haryana has regained its 'quit poverty' momentum but, in a paper prepared as recently as October 2001, Jeffery Sachs, Anupam Bajpai and Annabhi Ramiah have noted that following the Green Revolution high growth occurred in Punjab and Haryana and also, to a lesser extent, in other adjacent states of Rajasthan, Gujarat and Maharashtra, but populous eastern states like U.P. and Bihar failed to take advantage of Green Revolution and this factor can be regarded a cause of "divergence" or enhancement in inter-state inequalities during the Globalization process in India.

One of most visible manifestations of what one might call a "Globalization failure" pertains to the strategic front of inequalities, a failure which assumes great poignancy in the case of ROI since elimination of inequalities, individual a well as areal, was one of the most prominent items on the manifesto of its long "freedom struggle"; the Indian National Congress, which enjoyed pre-eminent dominance for the first four decades of the short ROI history and which is even now in control of as many as 14 states spread in all corners of its vast territory, is also committed to this goal making monitoring of the economic dispersion of the gains (and losses) of Globalization in terms of the territorial contours of the Indian political system an urgent necessity as the political parties which evolve the "correct" policies of public governance on this score is likely to gain better territorial acceptability.

Even the father of the nation Mahatma Gandhi, who was fond of and always emphasized for 'Swadeshi' set tone of globalization as early as in ***Young India, June 1, 1921***, when he said that "*I do not want my house to be walled in an all sides and my window to be stuffed. I want the cultures of all lands to be blown about my house as freely as possible. But I refuse to be blown off my feet.*"

Mr. Manmohan Singh advocated greater interaction with the world and warned that "if our economy is not equipped to absorb, assimilate, and to adopt this technical change which is taking place, all over the world, I think we will be marginalized. Many developing economies are already being marginalized in the new global economic system that has emerged."

If the prevailing political and administrative environment continues, the possibility of recurring crises in the near future is not ruled out. The symptoms have already started appearing. Sluggishness in exports in spite of gradual devaluation of rupee via open market, increasing fiscal deficit, downgrading in international credit rating of India, bearish trend in the stock market, non-preparedness of the Indian people particularly the elite to pay more taxes, etc., are signaling towards another crisis. Liberalization, privatization and globalization policies seem irreversible in India. India should strive to manage these mega trends to the best of its advantages.

Summing up

Human Development Report champions the agenda of the world's weak, those marginalized by globalization, and calls for a much bolder agenda of global and national reforms to achieve globalization with a human face. It cautions that globalization is too important to be left as unmanaged as it is at present, because it has the capacity to do extraordinary harm as well as good.

Liberalization, privatization and globalization policies have been exercising considerable influence on people and government. In developing countries like India, governance has responded both slowly and unevenly to economic liberalization. It is mainly due to the fact that liberalization policy in India has not evolved indigenously through the participation of political, bureaucratic and other institutions of governance. The liberalization policy is mainly adopted under the influence of World Bank – IMF combine. In case of India the institutions of economic governance have responded very quickly to economic liberalization. The post liberalization phase has witnessed amendments in many economic laws as well as introduction of economic laws to deal with changed environment.

Supremacy of economic institutions particularly finance ministry accompanied by erosion in the role of planning commission in economic policy making is another outcome of economic liberalization. Setting of new institutions such as Ministry of Disinvestments, Disinvestments Commission, Expenditure Commission and Regulatory Authorities in the field of telecom, power and insurance have increased the jurisdiction of economic administration in the Indian economy. Very fast growth of economic administration in response to liberalization, however, has not succeeded in achieving its goals such as a higher rate of growth on sustainable basis accompanied by improved efficiency and productivity in the Indian economy.

Further, these initiatives have covered mainly those services and areas, which cater to the elite. The areas of social concern such as poverty, unemployment, regional disparities and sectoral imbalance which have borne the burnt of liberalization policy have been kept out of these initiatives. This combination of coverage and neglect, if continued on the one hand would help the elite to consolidate its advantaged position and become partner of the ruling coalition of politicians and bureaucrats. On the other hand, it would alienate further the disadvantageous groups, sectors and regions from the mainstream.

Competitive markets may be the best guarantee of efficiency, but not necessarily of equity. Liberalization and privatization can be a step to competitive markets—but not a guarantee of them. And markets are neither the first nor the last word in human development. Many activities and goods that are critical to human development are provided outside the market—but these are being squeezed by the pressures of global competition. There is a fiscal squeeze on public goods, a times squeeze on care activities and an incentive squeeze on the environment.

In order to widen their policy options in the future and to strengthen their bargaining power, developing countries have to organize themselves to strive for a more democratic global system.

Grater collaboration among regional institutions of the South (for example, ASEAN, SAARC, SADC, Mercosur, Caricom etc.) especially in sharing of information and coordination of policies and positions, would be beneficial.

The developing countries should have more rights of participation in decision—making processes in the IMF, World Bank and WTO, which should also be made more accountable to the public and to the local and poor communities.

In the 21st century, much more focus has to be placed on changing economic policies and behaviour in order that the patterns of consumption and production can be made environmentally sound. What need to be discussed is not only the development model of the South but much more the economic model of the North and of course to international economic order.

There is also a need to strive for governance at a national level that combines economic development, environmental concern and social justice. In both North and South, the wide disparities in wealth and income within countries have to be narrowed. In a situation of improved equity, it would be more possible to plan and implement strategies of economic adjustment to ecological and social goals.

As globalization becomes the new mantra of the powerful on the planet with the unholy Trinity—the IMF, the World Bank, and the WTO— claming that it will solve all the economic problems of the world (including poverty and deprivation), it is time for the countries of Asia, Africa and South America to pause, take stock and critically appraise the whole process, examining the true and only options available to them.

The developing countries must be provided with a range of options regarding when, how and to what extent they should open their economics. For this, they must press their case in international forums and institutions where decisions on the global economy are made. Failure to do so would mean that they are subjected interminably to policies that further development prospects and options as well.

The developing countries should have more rights of participation in decision-making process in the IMF, World Bank and WTO, which should also be made more accountable to the public and to the local and poor.

There is also a need to strive for governance at a national level that combines economic development, environmental concerns and social justice. In both North and South, the wide disparities in wealth and income within countries have to be narrowed. In a situation of improved equity, it would be more possible to plan and implement strategies of economic adjustment to ecological and social goals.

We are aboard a train, which is gathering speed, racing down a track on which there are an unknown number of switches leading to unknown destinations. No single scientist is in the engine cab and there may be demons at the switch. Most of the societies are in the caboose looking backward.

BIBLIOGRAPHY

Adarsh Kishore,"*Globalization, Living Standards and Equity: Recent Progress and Continuing Challenges: National Experience – India,* Paper presented at the Workshop for G-20 Members, Sydney, May 26-28, 2002. Mimeo.

Ahluwalia, *The Economic Performance of the States in the Post-Reform Period"* in Rakseh Mohan (Ed.), Facets of The Indian Economy, New Delhi, OUP, 2002.

Alternative Economic Survey 2000-01, New Delhi, Alternative Survey Group, 2001.

A.S. Bhalla (Ed.), *Globalization, Growth and Marginalization*, London, Macmillan Press Ltd., 1998.

Beyer, P. (1994), *Religion and Globalization*, London, Sage Publications.

B. Ramesh Babu (Ed.), *Globalization and the South Asian State*, New Delhi, South Asian Publishers,1998.

B.R. Nayar, *Globalization and Nationalism: The Changing Balance in India's Economic Policy, 1950-2000*, New Delhi, Sage Publications, 2001.

Dieter Bos, *Privatisation: A Theoretical Treatment*. Oxford: Clarendon Press, 1991.

Dollar, David, *Globalization, Inequality and Poverty Since 1980*, Washington D.C. World Bank, Mimeo, 2001.

Eisenstadt, S.N. , *Modernization: Protest and Change*, Delhi, Prentice Hall, 1969.

Fukuyama, F., *The End of History and the Last Man*, New York, Free Press, 1992.

Hirst, P.Q. and Thompson, G., *Globalization in Question*, London, Cambridge, 1996.

Kurian, N.J., *"Widening Regional Disparities in India: Some Indicators, Economic and Political Weekly*, February, 12, 2000: 538-550.

Louis De Allesi, "The Economics of Property Rights: A Review of the Evidence", *Research in Law and Economics*, Vol. 2., 1980.

Magdoff, Harry (1992), *Globalization: To What End?*, New York, Monthly Review Press, 1992.

Peter Aucoin, *The New Public Management: Canada in Comparative Perspective*, Montreal, Canada: Institute for Research on Public Policy, 1995.

Prahlad, K. Basu *et al.*, *Governance and Government: Emerging Scenarios in the 21st Century* (Report for FCPC), New Delhi,1996.

Roberet, J. Holton, *Globalization and the Nation- State*, London, Macmillan Press Ltd., 1998.

Rostow, W.W., *The Stages of Economic Growth: A Non-Communist Manifesto*, London, Cambridge University Press, 1960.

UNDP, 1999, *Diversity and Disparities in Human Development: Key Challenges for India*, New Delhi.

V.S. Sheth (Ed.), *Globalization and Interdependence: Africa and India, Mumbai*, Allied Publishers Ltd., 2000.

World Bank, *World Development Report*, Washington D.C., World Bank, 2001.

10

Gandhiji's Views and Globalization

Prof. G. Ramachandrudu,
Dr. G.A. Prabhakar and A. Rajani

I do not want my house to be walled in on all sides and my windows to be stuffed. I want the cultures of all lands to be blown about my house as freely as possible. But I refuse to be blown off my feet by any.

—Mohandas K Gandhi

In this quotation Gandhiji expressed that India should not be confined its own culture rather to be open to all cultures of the world but should not be attracted to anyone. It seems we should adopt the cultures of whole world but should not be imitate any culture.

Market economy or globalisation is only for the well-to-do, a point Gandhiji might have overlooked. ***–Devarajan***

Objectives

The objectives of the study are:

1. To examine the views of Gandhiji on Globalization.
2. To explain the impact of Gadhiji international explores on his life and mission.
3. To suggest policy perceptive for India's progress in the context of Globalization.
4. Conclusions.

Various anti-globalization movements often ported that Gandiji has a different ideology, but he himself was a clear product of globalization. This can be understood by the life of Gandhiji. He was educated in London and started his political activity in South

Africa before he joined in Indian politics. He was greatly influenced by western figures like Jesus, Tolistoy, Thoreau and Ruskin. He identifies globalization as an ancient process and claimed that it was not a threat to India various races tried to invade India but evolved up by becoming a part of India. He believed that adopting different cultures in India would not be a threat to its own customs and culture. However, he warns that establishment of a global society may become a danger to sovereign nations in the form of colonialism, commercialization of economy leading to class antagonism and environmental hazards. Today, we see some of them in our daily liner, which says that Gandhi's relationship with globalization and his views are valid till date.

Gandhi was a firm between in keeping the ancient Indian culture and harms in our society. But with the integration of world community during the last 20th century, it can be argued that western influence affected India and many developing countries. Urban India today seem in the age of diet coke, flat screen televisions and super express highway. Crash diet, anti-wrinkle treatment. However, Gandhi says that Indian alternatives are in no-way inferior to Western.

He opined that globalization was not evil but to believe that everything western was superior was not the correct stand to take. He did not perceive any threat to our culture due to globalization but he did believe that it would lead to environmental hazards and consumerism—Ervils of liberal hegemony are also coming to the forefront—increasing inequality in countries embracing capitalism, huge balance of trade deficits tying up developing countries to western corporations and WTO/IMF norms leading to crisis and bankruptcy in many countries.

In such a scenario, Gandhi and his ideas on the economy are being hailed by many as the 'Third Way'—a suitable compromise between the leftists and free marketeers that ought to suit all classes. However, if we scrutinise Gandhian attitudes towards economics, we find a lot of similarities with both liberalism and communism. For instance, through the Swadeshi Movement, Gandhi advocated rejection of western textile and home spinning of cotton for Indians—this amounts to very much left wing protectionism which Nehruvian India adopted for over 35 years until under Dr. Manmohan Singh,

India began its journey to free market economics. Gandhi's views rested on the principles of co-operation and understanding—today it's more about competition and profit making. However, Gandhi's desire to safeguard peasants' rights seems valid even today.

Gandhi's movements to earn rights for Indians through strictly non-violent movements both in South Africa and India have been an invaluable component of the globalisation of the civil rights movement. For example, the strict adherence to non-violent means by Dr. Martin Luther King Jr., despite various provocations, portrays the depth of Gandhian beliefs in the American Negroes' civil rights movement.The Gandhian satyagraha was also adopted in South Africa firstly by the National Indian Congress and later personified by Nelson Mandela. In this age of violence, many of the most important civil rights movements throughout the world have been remarkably Gandhian in practice.

Globally, women have come to the forefront of developments in a much greater proportion, although they remain highly under-represented in the legislatures of most democracies, despite now having universal suffrage and rights as men. In India itself, the Women's Bill remains stuck in parliament to this day. Gandhi clearly defined the roles of men and women and defined women to be the dictator of domestic affairs while the man being the one to go out into the public sphere. This view has not only been overturned in the west, but also in India, whereby women are increasingly coming forward as equals of men in every sphere of life.

Conclusions

Thus, the crucial question facing us surely is—Are the notions of Gandhi and Globalisation contradictory? Not necessarily, it seems. Some of his ideas may seem utopian and unrealistic in the global society today, while others may seem in direct opposition to everything globalisation and liberalisation stands for. However, many of his principles remain valid even today and applied worldwide, the most notable being the principle of satyagraha. He brought forward practical issues facing the globalisation process today—that of environmental concerns, equality of rights for all, rural development and evils of violence. However, to sum up Gandhian attitudes towards globalisation as it stands today, it seems apt to conclude by quoting Kaviguru Ravindranath Tagore:

"We have for over a century been dragged by the prosperous West behind its chariot, choked by the dust, deafened by the noise, humbled by our own helplessness and overwhelmed by the speed. We agreed to acknowledge that this chariot-drive was progress, and the progress was civilisation. If we ever ventured to ask, `progress towards what, and progress for whom', it was considered to be peculiarly and ridiculously oriental to entertain such ideas about the absoluteness of progress. Of late, a voice (Gandhi) has come to us to take count not only of the scientific perfection of the chariot but of the depth of the ditches lying in its path."

The idea of trusteeship, among Gandhian ideas of social reconstruction, is the idea which has been or, one of those ideas which have been, considered to be impracticable. But it is also true that in his theory of social reconstruction the two building-blocks of which are non-violence (*ahimsa*) and truth (*satya*), practicalizing this idea could be the only logical way to stop capitalistic exploitation of labour. Gandhi had in his mind a picture of the way in which the political worker, the elected representative, that is, the political ruler, would or should, function in independent India.

Neither the Gandhian, nor the globalization, model raises any problem for ethical theory. Each one of them can be assessed, depending on the specificity of the context, in deontological, teleological, or virtue-theoretic terms, though generally theorists prefer to judge a development scheme in teleological, more specifically, utilitarian, terms. But the models do raise some problems for the ethics of development, that is, some practical, ethical, problems. This is clear from what has been said in earlier. It has been shown therein that the Gandhian model is more suited to ameliorating the conditions of the Indian poor, rural or urban, whereas the globalization model is more likely to benefit the urban, maybe even the rural, affluent. This is an ethical, or moral, difference between the two because it is more ethical to do the former than to do the latter, and therefore the Gandhian model is ethically superior to the globalization model.

Today world over NGOs are working along Gandhian principles to save and improve the environment and to spread peace through his works.

BIBLIOGRAPHY

Anto Akkara: *Learn from Gandhi: Anti-Globalisation Activists Urged* online at http://www.dfms.org/3577_26623_ENG_HTM.htm

Jan Oberg: In Birla House with Gandhi in 'Following Gandhi's Path Part 5' online at http://www.transnational.org/forum/meet/2002/fgp5_BirlaHouse.html

Mohandas Karamchand Gandhi: *Hind Swaraj and Other Writings* (Cambridge: Cambridge University Press, 1997).

Nelson Mandela: *Long Walk to Freedom: An-Autobiography* (London: Abacus, 2003).

Niranjan Ramakrishnan: *Whats so Great About Gandhi, Anyway?* in 'The Comprehensive Pursuit of Liberty' (October 2, 2003) online at http://www.counterpunch.org/ramakrishnan10022003.html

R. Sudarshan: *Globalisation and Gandhi at the Dawn of the Millennium in* 'General Discussion Forum for the RBAP-RR Meeting' (New Delhi: UNDP, 1998) online at http://rrmeet.undp.org.in/_disc8/00000002.htm

Stephen. B. Oates: *Let the Trumpet Sound: A Life of Martin Luther King Junior* (Edinburgh: Payback, 1998).

11

Engaging with Gandhi in Contemporary India

C. Shambu Prasad

Talk to students on the occasion of Martyrs Day (30th January, 2007) at the Centre for the Study of Gandhian Philosophy and Human Development, Gayatri Vidya Parishad Degree College, Visakhapatnam.

I have always been very ambivalent speaking about Gandhi and was hesitant when asked to speak on Gandhian philosophy. It is indeed difficult to speak about a man on whom so much has been written not just by others but by himself. One of the most documented persons in human history Gandhi gave a different meaning to the term 'probity in public life' and was courageous to treat his life as an open book by inviting us through his statement 'my life is my message'. Almost every incident of his has been documented, analysed, reinterpreted and open to revision. And yet there is no dearth of new information and insights on the person as also the controversies surrounding him. If the latest book by Rajmohan Gandhi (*Mahatma, A True Story of a Man, his People and an Empire)* raised controversies surrounding his alleged affairs, the not so creative video by a non-resident Indian in US raised a different kind of controversy. This soon after several news channels reported how Gandhi had become fashionable this year following the discovery of a new September 11, the start of Gandhi's satyagraha that was soon followed by the much celebrated film *Lage Raho Munnabhai*. I would like to begin this talk by this unique film that has caught the imagination of several youngsters in India and elsewhere. The film provided me an opportunity to revisit Gandhi without being diffident about my own ambivalence.

The movie has several caricatures of the way Gandhi has been used and abused by independent India and the comical satire carried was as effective as the earlier Munnabhai's satire on the medical profession that would have done Ivan Illich, the author of *Limits to Medicine*, proud. Apart from popularizing words such as Gandhigiri and reinterpreting Gandhi in local lingo, *bande mein tha dum* (the guy had tremendous courage) I think one of the things that the film has done which so many other films or books have not been able to achieve is to help us relate to Gandhi in a very personal sort of way. I recall several times going to seminar on Gandhi where the average age of participants would be over 65 each speaking about the importance of Gandhi to India and the world. I also witnessed how many Gandhians of a generation gone by were able to carry themselves so remarkably as well. We knew that they were no *khadi* kurta clad politicians but there seemed so much to mediate between the dishonest politician donning a *khadi kurta* and the Gandhi topi and the self-sufficient, non-violent Gandhian who lived the 'Gandhian way of life'. Murli Prasad Sharma, the underworld don in the film somehow brought Gandhi back to another sphere as a person with whom one could talk with, almost literally.

Lage Raho thus encourages me to be in the place of Murli Prasad Sharma and engage with Gandhi, if I may say on my terms—not as some Mahatma or Gandhiji 'out there' whom I have to constantly remember as a burdensome. Father of a very heavy nation state, but as a friendly Gandhi or Bapu with whom one can engage with on a continual basis. If some of you are expecting that I would propound Gandhian philosophy as some objective set of principles that are timeless and non-contextual I am sorry you might be in for a disappointment. On the other hand, I am hoping that by sharing my journey over two decades with Gandhi, Gandhism and Gandhigiri might help each one of you chart your own journeys in rediscovering Gandhi in contemporary India.

Before I embark on that journey I would like to share with you some facts about Gandhigiri. Many of you have perhaps been following how Gandhigiri has been interpreted by many citizens across India to raise their voice in a non-violent way so as to bring about change. The forms of protests have been remarkable and spontaneous from Lucknow where Gandhigiri was practiced to move a liquor shop from public places to Mumbai where citizens are protesting a construction company that cheated them. Public agencies have tried this out to influence errant road drivers. To this list I would like to share with you the wikipedia the open source encyclopaedia entry that states "People adopting Gandhigiri solve problems with perseverance, non-violence and tolerance (not having anger or hatred towards the ones you are opposing) rather than with violence. Gandhigiri aims to overcome 'Dadagiri' or 'bullyism' by encouraging people to adopt non-violent and constructive ways to solve a problem."[1] There are new campaigns on Gandhigiri with new websites where people have started sharing their views on societal change. One that I registered into, Gandhigiri.org had 720 members in the last 100 days with an impressive list of 740 postings and newer agendas added to the mission![2] Recently students in my own campus wore black caps to mark their protest amongst some of their own friends in what they perceived as an unfair placement atmosphere created by some of them.

While it would be easy to dismiss these happenings as something ephemeral and non-serious I think they need to be celebrated for what they are even if they are not exactly what Gandhi would have liked or followed or if they do not represent Gandhism in full measure. I would like to join in this qualified celebration of an interest in Gandhi by sharing with you a few more facts about *Lage Raho.* It was not nominated for the Oscars as you all know but few know that it was the first time that a Hindi film was ever screened at the UN.[3] Let me share with you an insight from the protagonist Sunjay Dutt. When asked if he had prepared for the film by reading Gandhi's experiments with truth his candid answer was no. He went on to add that he was able to learn about Gandhi from people around him—his parents who he felt had a lot of Gandhism in them.

II

I think we need to take Sunjay's invitation seriously and explore the Gandhi or Gandhism or Gandhigiri within us. *Lage Raho* made me realise something about myself and much like Murli Prasad Sharma, I too have had Gandhi come to me in very many ways even when I completely forget him or my involvement with his thoughts and action. Despite having read a lot about Gandhi and done a Ph.D on his views on science I have often found that speaking about Gandhian thoughts and action without referring to Gandhi is often very productive. People already have so many opinions about

Gandhi that you might end up in a conversation just chasing and deconstructing other people's opinions and perceptions about Gandhi before you can even speak about your own. He is one person everyone has an opinion about and there is an endearing quality about Gandhi that all of us can have such an opinion. As rightly observed by Ramachandra Guha in a recent interview on the controversy surrounding Gandhi's book by Rajmohan Gandhi, he is one person about whom you can say anything and not have your house burnt! That is something that we surely cannot do with other public figures such as Ambedkar or a Nehru or a Bose or legends such as Shivaji or even heroes such as Ganguly in certain parts of the country.

A friend once remarked, perhaps jocularly, that India's greatest export was not its software industry but Gandhi. I want to share with you this lovely experience I had of Bapu coming back to me during my first visit to Netherlands. I was on a flight from Maastricht to Amsterdam enroute India and my co-passenger was a stocky lawyer who was going to Surinam. I helped him with his seat belt and he started a conversation. He had never visited India and I had never before seen such a glow in anyone's face when they realised I was from India. To him India was not about elephants and poverty but the land of Gandhi and Krishnamurti. He shared with me his experience of watching the film Gandhi and how he was moved to tears. He believed that Gandhi's view as a lawyer was something that motivated him in his work. Today I can relate this incident to an almost private conversation with Bapu like Murli Prasad Sharma reminding me about the genuine truthful appreciation of certain universal values that Gandhi believed in and stood for. It is also a reminder for me when in doubt to recollect that there are more people practicing non-violence and have been influenced by Gandhian thought across the globe than we can imagine. Experiences of many have been documented and are often quoted but like this Dutch lawyer Gandhi has indeed touched so many people's lives in rather remarkable ways.

As a student and researcher on the Gandhian method it is a powerful reminder to steer clear from often futile and sterile debates on Gandhi that we witness over television at times and the argumentative Indian's (to use Amartya Sen's phrase) view on Gandhi. Not all Gandhians are brown, wear *khadi* and speak about

Gandhi. And so too the other corollary that not all neo-Gandhians, as Sunjay Dutt is now being called, needs to have read and memorised Gandhi's experiments with truth to be a Gandhian.

III

My journey with Gandhi however began in my teens with Gandhi's Autobiography, *My Experiments with Truth*. That is if one discounts what in retrospect were images that remained when I first read the Publications Division comic style strip on Gandhi's life that had the old man on the cover with a baby. I recall being impressed with the fact that Harischandra play had a lasting impact on Gandhi and that behind his mother's apparent passivity was a steadfast and powerful resolve expressed through the many vows that she undertook. The autobiography was one of the first books that I read. I was recovering from the grind and horrors of getting into IIT that often meant becoming a one dimensional human being with poor emotional quotient. Most south Indian IIT males could better relate to numbers and equations than people. Those from Andhra were worse, and as someone quipped 'kids in Andhra start by learning M CET before A, B, C'!

I was in hostel and recall doing at least two things then. Maintaining regular accounts of expenditure, starting a journal and a weekly fast (appropriately chosen when the food was particularly bad). Beyond this were of course the seed of belief in trying to live a truthful and non-violent life. This personal interest in Gandhi soon became began finding expression amongst a small group of peers with whom I was fortunate to grow up with. We had a set of friends who were not so keen on catching the first flight to US after graduation and were introduced to critical ideas on technology and development through a humanities course. One such friend from school was so influenced by *Hind Swaraj* the small booklet of Gandhi on India's Home Rule written in 1908 that he declared that he would devote his life to Hind Swaraj. Though not exactly an epitome of non-violence the sheer boldness and guts of Gandhi inspired him. That Gandhi could see clearly the futility of modern institutions such as parliament and even the modern professions and did not hesitate in using the choicest epithets to describe them touched a chord. He prior to that was thinking of industrial automation as a way out of child labour in Sivakasi and had contemplated journalism as a career as well. Another friend was inspired into taking to natural farming as a way of life. For many of us with an interest in environmental issues Gandhi seemed much ahead of time and inspired many environmental movements in India. His famous saying 'the Earth has enough to satisfy the need of all the people, but not for satisfying the greed of some,' cut at the heart of many environmental debates linking lifestyles and environmental health.[4]

None in our group claimed to be Gandhians though many of us still wear *khadi* or handloom cloth. The existence of a peer group was to me an important part in the exploration and engagement with Gandhi. We share common beliefs and interests in the Gandhian worldview of simplicity, effectiveness, courage, environmental ethic and practical action as important for social transformation. Our paths were different. One of us was fascinated with rural or village industries another with decentralised cotton spinning, a third with environmental action and others with Gandhi's thought. I later discovered similar groups of friends who formed active groups during their college days. One such was the Mysore Amateur Naturalists (or MAN) comprising of engineering students from Mysore in the late eighties. Within the group members specialised in grasses, snakes, birds, etc., even as they shared a dream of having land and farming differently. If one looks closely at Gandhi's life and times he too fashioned his ashrams whether in South Africa or India as places for eccentric refugees.

What I would like to emphasise here is that engaging with Gandhi to us and probably with many others was not an end in itself but an important starting point in discovering ourselves. We spoke with passion in activist meetings, opted out of regular jobs rather soon and often confronted senior Gandhians. We participated in the revival of Gandhian thought through a Chennai based think tank called the PPST Foundation (or the Patriotic and People Oriented Science and Technology) and started celebrating peoples knowledge and wisdom. I had by then completed my masters in industrial management and science policy and started work with an organisation working with craftspeople in Andhra. I was moved by articles in Frontline on starvation deaths of weavers in Andhra in the early nineties and was keen to join a group working on crafts and textiles. We had a lovely interaction with many activists and constructivists then. In the late eighties activists were those who worked for political change and constructivist were those who worked on building alternative visions on the ground. I was keen to engage with both simultaneously and was fascinated by accounts of Shankar Guha Niyogi of the Chattisgarh Mukti Morcha who I felt had parallels to much of Gandhian thinking though himself not a Gandhian. There were a few inspiring individuals such as the late Vinoo Kaley whom we met and worked with who could traverse both worlds and that fascinated me. Gandhi attracted me for his ability to combine these worlds so beautifully and in fact arguing that they never could be separate.

Coming from a middle class background and working with textiles Gandhi could not be too far. I was fortunate to work with colleagues who were open to a non-elite understanding of textiles and learnt a lot about natural dyes and hand spinning in Ponduru. As a group we spoke enthusiastically about 'Weaving a Vision' and shared a new understanding of textiles amongst Gandhians, textile designers and engineers as well. Gandhi by no means was universally accepted by all within our group. I perhaps more than many others remained loyal to Gandhian thought though much less to its action. We however had others who were more wedded to action, led the Gandhian simple life, wore only *khadi* and used local products and local knowledge often at some personal cost to ones own health, but had serious difficulties with Gandhi's ideas. There is something unique about the Gandhian method and way of being that you can be with or against Gandhian thought and action in some sort of 50-50 way. Few other thinkers place such high demands on theory and practice, ideology and action going together. Reflecting back on my close friend's discomfort with Gandhian ideas on non-violence I found that in some other sense he was actually much more of a Gandhian than me and vice versa.

Rajni Bakshi captured some of this new fascination for contemporary Gandhi in her book 'Bapu Kuti' and she had carried before the publication of the book several articles in *The Hindu* on people like us without branding us as Gandhians. Her book had a response that surprised many of us. Here were different lives from Aruna Roy's work with labourers in Rajasthan and the early seeds of the Right To Information struggle, Ganga Mukti Abhiyan, Seshadri the scientist, Baba Amte's vanaprastha, Ravindra Sharma the craftsperson, Karunakaran—the systems planner, Kumarappa's legacy along with our own story of Dastkar Andhra 'Weaving a Vision' combined into one book. Was it a sleight of hand or profound insight that linked Gandhi to all of us! The sub-title chosen by Rajni was 'Journeys in the rediscovery of Gandhi'. The book had a role to play in the making of the film *Swadesh* though Mohan Bharghav (played by Shah Rukh Khan) did not evoke the same response as Murli Prasad. For some readers like my Masters advisor and the teacher who floated the course technology and development, the book filled him with a sense of hope and optimism. It is not a coincidence that much of the idea for the book came to Rajni during the Kumarappa centenary celebrations and when at Sewagram or Bapu's Kuti. There is something about the Gandhian method that it has such diverse forms and not just the one drawn officially by Gandhians or our national historiographers. If I were to be poetic I would say it is in the air and one can smell it by scratching at the surface of many unrealities of public and personal life. I had by then scratched several such surfaces to merit a detailed study of Gandhi.

IV

It was during my work on indigenous textiles that I came back to Gandhi taking a more serious turn of a researcher. I began reading more and more of his writings through an interesting detour, namely through what has since been known as the cotton story. I was spending some time looking at archival material on cotton textiles from British records during independence and was documenting a rather fascinating story that emerged on Indian (de) industrialisation. We had as a group made links between the quality of cotton and hand spinning and weaving and discovered some historical evidence to show that Indian cotton was not inferior but that Indian processing techniques rendered even the short staple cotton such as Dacca and Ponduru into fabulous cloth. The same cotton though would be termed unspinnable in the modern textile science understanding of quality.

It was during that research I chanced upon *Young India*—a journal that ran from 1919 until 1931 and was edited by Gandhi and his co-workers. This was a collection that was always there in our library at IIT but was never touched by any of us. University curricula effectively bypass any engagement with Gandhi even as we are taught other thinkers. I began taking elaborate notes on cotton growing techniques and was absolutely fascinated that a primarily political journal actually carried with it articles that had details on how to revive India through hand spinning and the various techniques. Here was the technical and the social or political combined in one single frame. For those of us who grew up on modern western science that evolved out of separations of various kinds – fact and value, experiment and experience etc., this outlook was refreshingly bold and different. We began to see versions of social life that were possible without negating other spheres of life that allowed for dialogues between science and religion and politics as well. Gandhi was representing a worldview beyond the bi polar oppositions of secular and fundamental, where the combinations of science, religion and society could indeed be different without diluting each others contribution. Bhikhu Parekh the political philosopher who worked on Gandhi's political philosophy later wrote a lot on multiculturalism and one can argue that his insights on Gandhi's thoughts brings about possibilities in multiracial Britain that otherwise seem remote.

Coming back to technology and science, however, I realised glimpses of a different Gandhi from his works on *khadi*. I started reading on the other persons in the revival of *khadi* and came up with some very interesting discoveries. In my understanding of Gandhi, I was introduced to some fascinating insights by two eminent scholars – one a Gandhian and the other an anthropologist of science. The eminent scholar and historian Dharampal, who passed away recently, had some amazing insights on Gandhi and his ashrams. Shiv Visvanathan the anthropologist encouraged me in pursuing my research on the broader politics of textiles and who wrote this absolutely fascinating piece on Gandhi called reinventing Gandhi wherein he linked Gandhi to contemporary political debates and peoples movements. Shiv helped me look at Gandhi differently and I remember his one liner on Gandhi and science 'every citizen a scientist and every village a knowledge centre' and the 'ashram as a laboratory.' Dharampal provided me with some rather vital clues in Gandhi's way of organising people and his profound insights on the Indian way of thinking and being. I carried these ideas with me into my Ph.D work and had worked on a piece for the Economic and Political Weekly (EPW) called "Suicide Deaths and Quality of Indian Cotton: Perspectives from History of Technology and Khadi Movement."[5] The argument was that what we had painstakingly researched and arrived at through historical research linking various unconnected threads were actually discovered by the *khadi* movement not through theory but through its practice. Here was technology leading science and we as modern technologists and scientists ignoring these as backward and 'traditional'.

The libraries of Delhi were excellent places for study even as life in Delhi was inhospitable. Dharampalji's insights on Gandhi were amazing and he told us stories of Gandhi that we never knew. For instance Gandhi brought in radical changes in the way the Indian National Congress was organised making it remarkably democratic and broad based. Before his entry he told us how most of the funds of the Congress were spent in Britain raising awareness about India's case for freedom. Gandhi changed it by arguing that we should be doing much more in India to create change and then attention will follow us and need not be sought. His mass mobilizations and organisational genius were testimony to that possibility. Dharampalji would offer nuggets about the alienation of the Indian elite by Gandhi's action and how his amazing speech at Benares has to be curtailed because Annie Beasant thought it would offend the princes etc., or that Gandhi perhaps inspired so many people to start their own ashrams and societies for constructive work across the country and that these organisations were over a thousand in number. We rarely get to know these insights in our sanitized understanding of Gandhi. But what I consider even more tragic is the lack of research on Gandhian institutions. The Teen Murti library in Delhi has several microfilms on Gandhi's spinners association and village industries association, institutions that he formed to promote constructive work but while researching the *khadi* movement I was surprised to know that these were hardly researched. The meticulous minutes of every meeting of the All India Spinners Association (AISA) and other such Gandhian institutions are instructive for their levels of transparency, accountability and purposeful functioning that perhaps offers lessons for public administration and management. I wonder how many case studies can actually be worked from these resources!

Not all these were apparent to me so clearly then, I confess. I was however particularly interested in the way science was constructed in the *khadi* movement and if indeed there were lessons to be learnt from these for the way we our scientific institutions today function. However, we were taught that it is Jawaharlal Nehru to whom we need to look for when we speak about science. Gandhi, no way! A talk by India's leading scientist administrator Dr. Mashelkar at a Gandhi memorial lecture had almost nothing to say about Gandhi and science.[6]

It would be clear to you now that there were several thoughts buzzing around me when I was doing my research and let me tell you that not all researchers are as lucky as Murli Prasad Sharma who could, as it were, invoke Gandhi to solve their daily predicaments. However, I was very fortunate to interact with Prof. Swaminathan who had wide interests in several subjects such as Ajanta paintings, water management etc., as well as Gandhi. He had then written a booklet on Gandhi and was enthusiastic enough to buy the newly released CD-ROM of the collected works of Gandhi. He was kind enough to let me be its first user. I took to Gandhi's collected works with the enthusiasm that you would associate with the net savvy generation of today. Even without a proper search engine I was able to get leads into Gandhi's rich readings. I was interested in his views on science, innovation, technology, machine etc but ended up learning much more than that. Here was a person who could share profound insights on science and the future of the nation without experts' cueing him for the right words even as he would engage actively in discussions surrounding communalism or partition of India or untouchability. As a reader he invites and pushes you to break boundaries and disciplines. No reader of Gandhi's collected works can walk away with just one particular topic. Several compilations of Gandhi's writings exist and some very good ones are insightful but my experience has been that an engagement with the Collected Works at some point in time is like a pilgrimage that one needs to invest in.

One of the outcomes of this diligent search of the Collected Works was the compilation of Gandhi's views on science, technology and machine.[2] I shall not mention in detail Gandhi's views on science here, that might need another talk but I would like to mention a few things about the process. The first thing that I realised was that Gandhi's views were never fixed in time but constantly relating to the external environment. Many Gandhians have perhaps made the mistake of essentialising his thoughts in booklets on various subjects and have separated him from the context of his work. Where he said and to whom he said was as important as what he said. Thus I realised that in his writings we often ignored the very important contribution he had with his co-workers. Unlike what he said for outside consumption, in response to journalists from the West, the British and national leaders with whom he had disagreements, there was an equally large amount of material where he spoke to his co-workers on practical problems of how the new world needed to be shaped.[3] Having worked in the citizen sector trying to shape a new world I realised that these were indeed the critical insights lacking in the Gandhian literature and was thus thrilled to see a 'tentative' Gandhi engaging in tremendous detail on what would and would not work and how to go about it. In today's parlance this kind of engagement would be called 'knowledge management'. However, it is perhaps strange that there have indeed been so few studies on how knowledge was actually managed by Gandhi and others.

The effort Gandhi spent in preparing his country for freedom has often been underestimated. In this he worked very hard in educating and making critical thinkers and doers of his own countrymen and never fought shy of learning from others. A lesser known fact about Gandhi is his effort to chronicle the lives of great people in his journal *Indian Opinion* that he edited while in South Africa. He wanted to build his countrymen for courage and non-violence even though they were otherwise living conditions close to bondedness without basic human rights. It is in this process that Gandhi was often very critical of traditionalists, a fact belied by his outward looks and demeanour. I discovered this while reviewing his writings on Ayurveda. But importantly this questioning of tradition was from the position of a critical insider with a view to exhort his countrymen towards better scientific research and contemporary relevance. He would offer them the examples of the spirit of modern scientists who he admired and who he felt were never shy of experimenting with themselves. This ability and need to experiment with the self is indeed his important contribution to the scientific method, a tradition that has been ignored in the west even though scientists like JBS Haldane after Gandhi have since keen to pursue subjects such as a 'non-violent biology.'

Modern science has externalised many aspects of life and we remain disconnected with what economists call 'negative externalities'. Gandhi pushes us to explore beyond the immediate environs of the laboratory, the corporation etc., to bring the 'other' –

the dumb creatures of life on whom vivisection is practised, the tribal and peasant whose lives are impacted often negatively by development and economic growth. The balance sheets of Coco Cola would never reflect the irreversible damage caused to village communities in Plachimada in Kerala or Mehdiganj in UP where groundwater is extracted at rates to fill the supposed thirsts of middle class India. In Gandhi's science these could not be disconnected and we realised that he was making these exhortations not just as an arm chair academic of philosopher but in the context of finding and being involved in alternative worldviews. He encouraged his fellow country men to be scientific and innovative in ways that modern India has indeed forgotten. The forms of organisation he chose to propagate his thinking were very modern. He made efforts to create scientific communities within the *khadi* movement, announced prizes for improved machines and made his co-workers write books and new texts in an otherwise ancient tradition of craft knowledge and oral traditions. In his writings he asked Indians to reflect on why Indians had not produced inventors that Britain had during the industrial revolution and encouraged Indians to respect working and thinking with hands.

The collected works though need to be seen not in isolation. I spent a fair amount of my time on Gandhi for my thesis but was looking and seeking other stories and accounts of other actors. One such, my favourite and under-celebrated Gandhian is Maganlal Gandhi. Few of us know about Maganlal who died in 1928 and thus most living Gandhians too have no memory of this amazing person who was with Gandhi through his struggles in South Africa and a key hand in setting up Gandhi's famous ashrams. It is important for us to spare a thought for Maganlal today even as the country, or the Congress party, celebrates the centenary of Satyagraha in South Africa through an international conference.[9] Few know that it is to Maganlal's credit that the word satyagraha was coined. Maganlal had suggested *Sadagraha* that Gandhi later worked on to Satyagraha. Gandhi's tribute to Maganlal is one of the most moving tributes by him and was titled 'My Best Comrade Gone'. A tribute that would have done most communists proud. I had a chance of discovering this relationship and documenting it and must confess that it was not 'newsworthy' as Gandhi's relationship with Sarladevi! I was of course called for a seminar on Gandhi and his contemporaries at Simla in 1999 but I think I had greater satisfaction sharing the insights with an old Gandhian Jyothibhai Desai than from any academic or media approval.[10] I share this because I believe that a serious engagement with Gandhi will soon have to look at uncharted territories and not all of these are likely to succeed or make us into heroes. But then the stress on means is something that Gandhi encourages us to engage with. He never for instance approved of any separation of ends from its means and pushed himself and humanity to search for and be creative in the application of the means of action.

One of the techniques of action that Gandhi has encouraged in India and elsewhere is the extension of Satyagraha or 'passive resistance' into Non-Violent Direct Action of NVDA. Murli Prasad Sharma and those inspired by Gandhigiri are actually in the business of NVDA. NVDA is serious business for several organisations from Gandhian institutions, *Narmada Bachao Andolans* and many other peoples movements to even international organisations such as Greenpeace where these methods have been researched and refined and are thought. It is probably one of India's greatest export in recent times, an export that is open source and has been refined, improved and applied several times over across the globe. Gene Sharp of the Albert Einstein Institute and a remarkable non khadi clad Gandhian lists at least 198 historical instances of use of NVDA in history and styles of following non-violent action.

I hope I have given you a flavour of the kinds of engagements possible with Gandhi often not even using his name. Gandhigiri is just one of them. For students and researchers Gandhi offers enormous opportunities for research and study for his views are invariably, if read and interpreted carefully, likely to offer insights on several issues. I have over the years looked at the Collected Works as a resource to learn about Gandhi's views on business organisations and the role of democracy, understand social entrepreneurship etc. I would like to now spend some time on how you could perhaps apply them in your own life and in contemporary India

V

A justifiable criticism of LRMB was that it says nothing about rural India except for the lovely joke by Arshad Warsi or Circuit on his having to go back to his village and plough the land and thereby making the cattle unemployed. Apart from Gandhi's sweep in thinking and action that has a civilisational canvas of science, democracy and the middle class, one of Gandhi's lasting contribution was to make modern India think and reflect about the other India or what he called the real India. India to him lived in its villages. Thus to Gandhi an Indian has as much to worry about farmers suicides, jobless growth even as it celebrates itself as the new knowledge superpower providing unheard of opportunities for its burgeoning middle class. The *khadi* movement was about freedom of India as Nehru rightly called *khadi* the 'livery of freedom' but it was also about how middle class India needed to connect with the large hinterland and relate to its problems. An engagement with Gandhi ignoring rural India means voting for a society with a lot of strife and unrest in the years to come. Arundathi Roy rightly described the pursuit of development involving displacement of so many rural Indians from their homes and means of livelihood as a 'fury that is building up across the country'. Few of you know that in neighbouring Orissa a highway has been blocked by rural Indians who lost their lives in police firing at Kalinga Nagar objecting to the takeover of their land by the Tatas. There are so many Kalinga Nagars in the making and we have in pursuit of numbers of double digit growth etc., forgotten Gandhi's talisman—'Whenever you are in doubt, or when the self becomes too much with you, apply the following test. Recall the face of the poorest and the weakest man [woman] whom you may have seen, and ask yourself, if the step you contemplate is going to be of any use to him [her]. Will he [she] gain anything by it? Will it restore him [her] to a control over his [her] own life and destiny? In other words, will it lead to swaraj [freedom] for the hungry and spiritually starving millions? Then you will find your doubts and your self melt away." The talisman that he gave us in 1948 has often been forgotten not once but several times by our governments, businessmen and technocrats. We indeed live in a world where we are unfortunately separated from the rural poor that we perhaps cannot even remember his/her face.

Connecting with rural India is indeed a challenge but luckily for us there are excellent examples to learn from. Organisations such as Sodhana in Vizianagarm district and the inspiring work of Dr. P. D.K. Rao is a place that you could visit and explore how villages have been transformed silently over the years. As a city bred person I remember the great learning that me and my friends had when we as students visited remote Dharmapuri district as part of a 'Discover India' workshop and we stayed in villages experiencing the joy and sorrows of rural India even as we were engaged in an energy survey in the village. We learnt a lot about ourselves too as a result. Many organisations now make this part of the curriculum and not just as NSS or National Service Scheme. For instance at our institute we have a 'Rural Living and Learning Experience' where our current rural management students have been sent across eastern India. It would be a good idea to explore Gandhi not only through visits to Sewagram but also through taking up some sort of work in neighbouring villages or even in the city of Visakhapatnam as you pursue your studies.

In one of the insights provided by Shiv Visvanathan in his reinventing Gandhi, he remarks how Gandhi today would have not gone to England but to America and would have been an engineer rather than a lawyer, like Mohan Bharghav in Swadesh. I suspect most of you in this generation are net savvy and it must come as no surprise to you that much activism today is through the internet with so many blogs and websites on virtually anything. But I would like you to engage with so many neo Gandhians who have been concerned about rural India. There are several Indians who have in recent years related to India more strongly after they have gone abroad, away from their parental anxieties in rediscovering themselves and India as well. Some of them have formed excellent groups and networks and I shall share with you a few examples. The Association for India's Development or AID is an excellent network of Indians interested in change in rural India.[11] One of its founders Sandeep Pandey was offered the Ramon Magsasay Award. Groups such as AID has brought remarkable dynamism to Indian activism and you can register with many of their mailing lists and through them learn about their campaigns and participate as well. I have often felt sorry that so few Indians from India participate in their signature campaigns. But better still it is important to move from 'virtual activism' to engaging with real people in real time and it would be a great idea to invite some of them to share their experiences and journeys. You could also visit the chapter closest to you in Orissa at Parlakhemundi where some exciting work is on rural technology, alternative education etc. The numbers I assure you are not small and you would do well to combine classroom learning, net based learning with visits to various parts of India to experience India differently and inviting people to share their experiences. You could also learn from their experiences to form your own groups to learn further on topics of contemporary relevance.

To share with you an example I came across an interesting study group called Sangati based in Chennai. The Sangati Learning Session is conducted "to understand and create awareness about ongoing social initiatives in Chennai by individuals and organisations. Themes explored include health, education, child rights, gender, environment, peace, dalit rights, land rights movements, education etc. These sessions are a monthly activity of the Chennai Branch of Sangati, a budding volunteer driven organisation in India and USA aiming to promote social action with deep understanding of self and society." The list of learning sessions that they have had and the speakers is indeed impressive and I see no reason why you cannot start something similar in Vizag. Further, it would be a good idea to have some of these networks discussing things in Telugu. The city and the region that it represents has I am sure several eminent personalities who can share their experiences. One such individual I would strongly recommend is Venu Madhav Govindu who was from Vizag but is currently engaged in a very interesting engagement with Gandhi, namely an authoritative biography of Kumarappa—the economist and thinker who took forward much of Gandhi's thoughts during and after independence. Kumarappa was one of the few dissenting voices then on the path pursued by independent India.

Either way I think it would be a good idea for you to reflect individually and collectively in small groups and then seek to move beyond your college to explore Gandhian philosophy in practice. I would like to leave you with just one quote from Dr. Abhijat Joshi the scriptwriter of LRMB. In an interview he recounts his journey on the making of Munnabhai and remarks, "Just one film will not make corruption or superstitions vanish. But it will start a debate. When people engage in debate, it creates an ambience through which eventually these things are confronted. If Charles Dickens had not written *Oliver Twist*, child labour may have continued longer. It did not put a stop to child labour in the 19th century England but it started something."[12] So too I hope this talk would indeed help you engage in a debate and with Gandhi and you enjoy the journey as much as I have over the years. I hope I have provided you with sufficient glimpses of how I have engaged with Gandhi and how you too could in your own future. I look forward to hearing about your first Gandhigiri initiative in the near future.

REFERENCES

1. http://en.wikipedia.org/wiki/Gandhigiri.
2. One is reminded of Shahid Amin's book on the Chauri Chaura incident on how Gandhi's call for non-violence was reinterpreted to mean so many diverse things that Gandhi perhaps never intended. See Amin, Shahid, 1995. *Event, Metaphor, Memory*, New Delhi: Oxford University Press.
3. Another website seeks to post case studies on Gandhigiri after LRMB. see www.gandhigiri.co.in
4. For a recent understanding of these debates see Ramachandra Guha's latest book *How Much Should a Person Consume*, New Delhi: Permanent Black.
5. Shambu Prasad C., 1999, Suicide Deaths and Quality of Indian Cotton: Perspectives from History of Technology and Khadi Movement. January 30, Jan. 30-Feb. 5. PE 12-21.
6. See Mashelkar R A. 2001. *Building Borderless Minds and Borderless Thinking*. Mahatma Gandhi Memorial Orentiation at the Indian Institute of Management, Kolkata, 16 October. http://www.csir.res.in/csir/external/heads/aboutcsir/leaders/DG/dgsp2.pdf.
7. This was part of my thesis and came out in EPW. Shambu Prasad C., 2001. "Towards an Understanding of Gandhian Science." *Economic and Political Weekly*, Sept. 29, 3721-32.
8. I am thankful to Dharampalji for his valuable insight that Gandhi had by the early thirties been assured of freedom and was actually more concerned with independent India and the preparation for that. He was in this and many other instances well ahead of the Congress leaders.
9. See http://www.satyagrahaconference.com/introduction.asp for details.
10. For a good biography of Maganlal and his relation with Gandhi See Shambu Prasad C., 2002. "Gandhi and Maganlal: Khadi Science and the Gandhian Scientist." In Bindu Puri ed. *Mahatma Gandhi and his Contemporaries*. Shimla: Indian Institute of Advanced Studies.
11. See www.aidindia.org for details.
12. Rediff interview with Abhijat Joshi http://www.rediff.com/movies/2006/sep/26joshi.htm.

12

The Challenges Posed by Mahatma

Dr. Madhu

The 30th of January returns once more reminding us of the person we all refer to as the father of the nation. We declared his birthday a national holiday, erected statues all over the country, named hundreds of roads after him and hung up his portraits in thousands of government buildings and felt that we could relax. Nevertheless a nagging fear persisted that we had still not done full justice to him.

For a while we remembered that somewhere he had spoken about the poor and so we loudly proclaimed that after *angrez hatao* (remove foreigners) we will take up the task of *garibi hatao* (remove poverty). Soon we discovered that *garibi hatao* was too intractable a task so we thought garib hatao would do just as well. If poverty could not be eliminated it could at least be put out of sight. As time went by we decided to abolish the word poverty itself and decided to build or not to build grandiose temples, to buy huge aircraft carriers, to send or not to send our own satellite to the moon. These are some of the issues that now occupy our attention.

This paper is based on the articles written by Homer A. Jack, peace activist (Darshan, Vol. Six, October 1989), Mark Lindley (Sarvodaya, Vol.1, No.5, Jan-Feb., 2004), Kanti Mehta, and Dr. Ravindra Kumar (Mahatma Gandhi and Higher Education: A Critical Analysis).

Mohandas K. Gandhi was a great Gujarati, an outstanding Indian and the Father of the Nation. He was a noble Asian and a distinguished Hindu. More than all of these, Gandhi was a great human being. Gandhi overshadowed many great people (Churchill,

Roosevelt, Lenin, Mao, Nehru, Einstein and Freud). As world citizen, he influenced and even after his death he has a continuing influence on dozens of movements and millions of people even today. Gandhi was not a philosopher. He was a man of action. He is the closest we have to a worldwide model of a good person from the last several centuries.

Contribution of Gandhi

Gandhi's basically talked of peace, non-violence and truth, of a society based on love and not hate, of the importance of the village where the bulk of the Indian people live, of the decentralization of the power structure, of the removal of social ills like untouchability, and of the importance of organic farming.

The Mahatma (great soul) had a vision of India — an India where diverse cultures would exist side by side in harmony like flowers of different hues in one fragrant bouquet and where the touchstone for every action would be the effect it would have on the poorest of the poor. There were some who did not like this idea. They assassinated him. The very forces that murdered him are finding that they had destroyed the body, but had failed to destroy his thoughts and his teachings which are still attracting and offering hope to millions of our countrymen. Even more terrifying for them is the strange phenomenon being witnessed the oppressed and the persecuted all over the world are finding in the Mahatma's ideas the weapon that they need to pursue their struggle for freedom and dignity.

Gandhi's Ideas in Contemporary World

Gandhi lives today in dozens of fields of Endeavour.

Satyagraha

It is alive today wherever conflicts are being resolved-peacefully. Satyagraha-non-violent direct action of soul force was Gandhi's great contribution to humanity.

It is being studied and used in many parts of the world today. Since Gandhi's death, there have arisen an American Gandhi (Martin Luther King Jr.), a South Korean Gandhi (Jam Son Hon), a Palestinian Gandhi (Awad Mubarak), and several others. Gandhi's name was mentioned during the student demonstration in Beijing's Tiananmen Square and non-violent direct action has been intentionally used against apartheid in the defiance campaign of 1952 and again in the last few months. (Gandhi devised these techniques during his 26 year sojourn in South Africa, ending in 1914).

Simple, Healthy and Intentional Life

Gandhi is relevant wherever people want to such lives.

Gandhi's ashrams in South Africa and India were experiments in simple living, prototypes to "small is beautiful." Gandhi remains relevant for the growing Green movements throughout the world, for ecological awareness, for healthful foods (as well as vegetarianism).

Religious Harmony

Gandhi's ideas become relevant where great world religions try to heal and not divide, where Hindus meet Muslims, where Christians dialogue with Jews.

Gandhi's prayer meetings have become a model for multi-religious meditation today. Also such international groups as the World Conference on Religion and Peace owe their origin, at least in part, to Gandhi's concept of religious dialogue as well as to his inspiration.

Disarmament and Peace

Gandhi is alive in every deliberation of negotiation for disarmament and peace. Wherever war and violence is abhorred and questioned, Gandhi is present. He lived 29 months into the nuclear age, asserting, "Unless new the world adopts non-violence, it will spell certain suicide for mankind." He early demanded disarmament. His call for unilateral disarmament was, after his death, tried by Secretary Khrushchev and President Kennedy, and then by President Gorbachev. His inspiration aided the great peace marches and demonstrations of our time, east and west, and his picture was often carried by those marchers.

Gandhi is Everywhere

Gandhi statues, Gandhi museums, Gandhi exhibits, Gandhi motion pictures, Gandhi plaques – all are important symbols so that a new generation can remember Gandhi.

The Collected Works of Gandhi, now in 90 volumes, makes Gandhi's word available to all. Many volumes continue to be published about Gandhi, worldwide, including children's books. Thus his insights are alive in the hears of countless persons of all ages, in all walks of life, in all climes and countries, perhaps as much outside India as in India itself.

Yet India cannot keep Gandhi for itself. He was a world figure; he remains one, the best the 20th century has produced.

Albert Einstein said it well: "Generations to come will scarce believe that such a one as this ever in flesh and blood walked upon this earth."

Self-Discipline

Gandhi's first set a challenge for himself; to exercise strong self-discipline. He did it in many ways.

He dressed very simply, and shaved his head.

He didn't go to concerts or the theatre.

One whole day every week he refrained from speaking. He did physical work a couple of hours everyday. (And to do that was a condition which he set for every able-bodied person wishing to live in his experimental commune. What a healthy idea that was!).

His eating was much disciplined: not only was he a vegetarian, but also on each day he would take only five articles of food, and none after sunset.

He and his wife took, at the age of 36 or 37, a vow of chastity, and then kept it.

And, with the consent of their four children (but contrary to her wish) de declined to keep any money or material property for them to inherit.

Gandhi thrived on all that discipline—he was naturally so inclined to excess that he needed a lot of self-discipline in order to function well.

In his later years he would advise his friends not to overdo it but instead to know themselves and to tailor accordingly their undertakings in self-discipline.

He would tell them, for instance, not to take a vow unless they were sure they could keep it.

"One reason, very important to him, why he declined to live like an upper middle-class person – which he could readily have done, since he had a successful law practice in Johannesburg and after moving back to India could have had one in Bombay is that it would have alienated him from the millions of poverty stricken people in India whom he wished to serve and to lead.

Non-Violence

Gandhi's concept and use of non-violence were more sophisticated – less absolute and more elaborate – than many people realize.

Already in his childhood he had known some Jain monks (Jains were so absolutely non-violent that in order to avoid inadvertently killing a mosquito or a worm they would wear veils over their mouths and not walk outdoors at night).

Gandhi rejected that mentality unequivocally. He said: "The emphasis laid on the sacredness of sub-human life Jainism is understandable. But that can never mean that one is to be kind to this {sub-human} life in preference to human life. ...To benefit by others" killing {of sub-human creatures} and delude oneself into the belief that one is being very religious and non-violent is sheer self-deception. ....In life it is impossible to eschew violence completely. The question arises, where is one to draw the line?...{For instance} to allow crops to be eaten up by animals in the name of *ahimsa* {loving non-violence} while there is a famine in the land is certainly a sin. Evil and good are relative terms. What is good under certain conditions can become an evil or a sin under a different set of conditions.

The challenge was to refrain not only from violence but also from deception, hatred, sarcasm (because it might interfere with the essential reaching out into the antagonist's soul) and any extraneous pressure on the antagonist.

A classical example of this last point is his decision in South Africa in 1914 to suspend an ongoing campaign of mass civil disobedience, because the railroad workers had suddenly called a big strike and the police would have been overburdened to handle both groups simultaneously. General Smuts's secretary told Gandhi:

> "You help us in our days of need. How can we lay hands upon you? I often wish you {Indians} took to violence like the English strikers, and then we would know at once how to dispose of you. But you will not injure even the enemy. You desire victory by self-suffering alone and never transgress your self-imposed limit of courtesy and chivalry. And that is what reduces us to sheer helplessness."

Urbanisation

Gandhi prophetically warned about the dangers of crores of people living in densely packed towns. The growing concentration of people in towns and cities as a result of urbanization (now regarded as an index of progress) and the ever widening gulf between the few very rich land the many very poor has resulted in a milieu in which crime, drugs, violence, exploitation of women as a commodity, growing incidents of rape and murder of women, are a regular feature of urban life. And this is a phenomenon which is not peculiar to India but is prevalent the world over. The larger the city, the greater the incidence of crime, violence and the other attendant ills and vices of urban society.

Present Day Colonialism

Colonialism in the sense of exploitation of one country by another through political control may have disappeared with the break up of the old Empires, but "the colonial system is however still practiced in its essence by countries aspiring to effect a quick entry into the modern era vis-a-vis their own rural population. Industry imposes manufactured goods on the villages in quantity and at the price it desires and makes them produce raw materials in the quantity and at the price the industrialist wants."

Social Order and World Peace

Gandhi was sensitive even to the danger that his own exalted reputation-since most people in India were saying and believing the kind of thing about him that Einstein in American said in 1945 – could hinder their capacity to think clearly in 1946 Gandhi said: "I ask nobody to follow me. Everyone should follow his or her own inner voice. If he or she has no ears to listen to it, he or she should do the best he or she can {and} in no case imitate other sheep like."

A social order founded upon vigorous self-governing communities of peasant-craftsmen, Gandhi held, would prove a veritable bulwark of democratic freedom and provide a natural guarantee against any aggressive or expansionist tendency on India's part. It would be a tremendous asset to world peace.

It is not worth pondering over today when increasing reliance on arms including nuclear weapons has caused tremors in the world and isolated us from the overwhelming majority of people and countries who genuinely desire peace and refuse to accept that the way to peace is through bigger stockpiles of arms and missiles equipped with nuclear weapons.

Environmental Concerns

Gandhi's ideas about the importance of organic farming and the dangers of using chemical fertilizers sounded weird and impartical at the time he propounded them. Till the forties ecology and environment were not issues that were considered worth worrying about in India.

Gandhi's ideas on the need for a cattle based rural economy were ridiculed as a reversion to the 'cow-dung' era and 'bullock cart mentality' and even as a reversion to medievalism. Today when in the developed countries of Europe and America a powerful movement against the use of chemical fertilizers has emerged and when in some countries such as Germany import of food products not bearing the green label (as a guarantee that no chemical fertilizers of pesticides have been used in heir production) is banned we need to realize that far from a reversion to medievalism Gandhi was far ahead of his times.

"Earth provides enough to satisfy every man's need but not for every man's greed" said Gandhi. So long as we cooperate with the cycle of life, the soil renews its fertility indefinitely and provides health, recreation, sustenance and peace to those who depend on it. But when the predatory attitude prevails, nature's balance is upset and there is an all round biological deterioration. Do all these Gandhian ideas smack of medievalism? Are they not rather post-modernist and prophetic? Today more than half a century after his martyrdom and after our rejection of his ideas, is not what is happening in our country and large parts of the world exactly as he had warned?

Today international conferences are being convened to debate how the alarming deterioration of the world's environment, which has not only turned once fertile areas in to dust bowls, which is also changing the world's climate and threatening the very existence of life on this planet, can be arrested. In a desperate bid to try to eat the cake and have it there is talk of sustainable development which is only an attempt to carry on exactly as are doing and only add some pollution control machines to control the damage. This of course incidentally provides opportunities to manufacturers of pollution control equipment to profit from the all round pollution that is taking place.

In the last few years we have seen a big out cry in the media and in the parliament because tests have revealed that the levels of pesticides and other chemicals in the bottles of the world's two most famous companies marketing soft drinks were above the limits required to make them fit for and safe for human consumption. Considering the clout of these companies it is unlikely that any real change will be effected to improve the quality of the drinks. Meanwhile, there are already attempts being made to counter the public concern over the matter by pointing out that all our vegetables and fruits, almost all the water available in the country and even the fish and meat contains residues of chemicals that are hazardous for human consumption, which is of course true, because fertilizers, pesticides and chemicals are being used for the production of all our food and these are sinking into the soil; and polluting the rivers and even our underground water tables. Clearly there is no short cut solution to the problem of the deterioration of the environment; it is only the long and dusty road back to the ideas of the Mahatma that can lead us to safety.

Education

Mahatma Gandhi stressed that education should not be limited to gain literary knowledge, but should include the moral, physical and mental development of a person.

In courses of time, education has to develop a person in all respects in order to enable him to become self-reliant. A man cannot make an all-round progress of cannot be self-dependent on the basis of any of the qualities of intellect, and physical or spiritual development. To become self-dependant or for his all round development, it is necessary that he should have moral upliftment in addition to his physical or intellectual development. It is absolutely necessary that he should not only be able to earn his bread, but should be able to fulfill the obligations of his family; and carving the path of his progress should ultimately be able to achieve his goal of life. This statement by Mahatma Gandhi's is entirely true even in the context of the world.

Colleges

Mahatma Gandhi had talked about self-sufficiency of colleges and universities. It meant that these institutions instead of depending on the government-aid should be self-financed.

India is an agricultural country. Most of the industries are based on agriculture. Gandhi wanted that more and more self-financed Agriculture-Colleges should be opened and they should be attached to related industries which would turn out graduates according to their requirement. Not only this, they should bear the expenses of their education and the training staff.

Gandhi wanted the same system to be adopted for the engineering or medical graduates. The engineering graduates should be attached to the related industry and the medical graduates to hospitals. The Law, Commerce and Arts colleges can be managed by the voluntary organisations and donations can be procured according to their requirement. Mahatma Gandhi was never in favour of government-aid. He, however, wanted the universities' control over the colleges and that of the government over the universities.

It is another matter that under the present circumstances, we have not been able to incorporate his views in our system of higher education, but they are worth giving a thought. The self-dependence he has talked about is certainly significant, otherwise how long will the colleges and the universities thrive on government-aid? Keeping lit in view, we will have to make a firm and well planned schedule and put jilt into practice.

13

Relevance of Gandhi: The Need for "Peoples Movement of Gandhian Alternatives"

K.S. Sastry

Mahatma Gandhi had shown us the path of Sarvodaya, Vinobha placed at before the country with new intensity and urgency in the form of the comprehensive vision of Gramswaraj.

Te decay, as one experience now-a-days, is eating into the vitals of developing nations very fast. Neither capitalism nor communism could stop it.

In our country, our political system that has become most ineffective and most brutal, and our national economy is gasping for breath in coils of multinational companies with the backing of the new economic policy.

Today the developed nations are pushing the poor developing countries into the cess-pool of poverty and misery, ignorance and ill-health, instead of helping to alleviating poverty and increasing employment potential.

Technology

The modern and high technology has come to be raised to the status of an ideology. All problems of humanity can be solved through; technology and without it no, society can progress or develop. The newer the technology, the better it must be. This is the ideology, Modern and high technology started first with the conveyor bet system. Then came automation and now computarisation is the latest thing. For cutting costs of production and reducing work-force and labour problems, the ultimate thing in this line is the robot-technology which does not need rest, food or sleep, does not form trade-unions or demand-raises in wages. Gandhiji described the evil nature of this greed based craze for machinery for personal enrichment.

Development

A great misconception of global dimension is continuing since decades, it is a pure illusion that the life style and the industrial and market systems adopted by the nations of the North/West is the right pattern of development.

We have only recently begun to realize that the present mode of development is causing widespread and great damage to the environment and to the entire eco-system of the planet. Pollution of air, water-streams and even of the seas and destruction of forests and of the diverse species of flora and fauna and of the habitats of large masses of the people are rampant. Bloated metro policies in which majority of the people live in slums without elementary civic services, beef contaminated with the mad-cow disease, reducing cattle and animal population by introducing abattoirs damage to the Ozone layer, global warming etc., are diverse instances of the consequences of the present mode of development. Many more can be cited. Development, however, rushes headlong without really bothering about the trail of destruction it leaves behind so long as the market yields profits.

Blind pursuit of wealth, profits and the goodies of life has spawned crime, drug-smuggling and addition, gang wars, land grabs, extortion, kidnapping and adduction, large and mega scams of all kinds, corruption of the highest levels and crime rampant and against women. Child prostitution and sex tourism get acceptance as a part of this development process. All moral and ethical values are fast falling and changing to the social values upheld by western civilization. This model of development based on financial-capital-intensive, exploitative and harmful technologies will have to be rejected totally, if we desire a change towards a healthy sustainable growth and society.

Gandhian Alternatives

Sarvodaya and Gramswaraj envisaged by Gandhi and Vinobha, are for the growth and development based on:

1. Non-Violent and non-exploitative and self-reliant.
2. Non-Polluting decentralized technology and non-centralized technology.
3. Development of growth without destruction, and eco-friendly.
4. Not global competition but global coordination.
5. Egalitarian society and panchayat powers
6. Employment intensive and not financial capital-intensive.

So, let all the right-thinking people and GANDHIANS come together to pull the country to Sarvodaya and Swaraj; oppose the uncontrolled powers, or global and national capital. The present process of globalization is artificial and unsustainable. It is not irreversible as ideological propaganda tries to make the people believe.

Gandhian Alternatives alone can fill-up the vacuum created by the failures of capitalism and communism. Thus Gandhi is more relevant in 21 century than at any other-time.

TO QUOTE MANMOHAN CHOWDHARY, "The world is groaning under the yoke of neo-imperialism. There will be no peace, prosperity."

A Gandhian Approach to Intergrated Rural Development

Appropriateness of any development in science and technology, whether Western or indigenous, big or small, traditional or non-traditional, is mainly attributed to its suitability to the prevailing peculiar situations and its efficacy in solving the serious problems confronted by the people and the country.

In a developing country like India, whose population may reach over 1000 million (100 crores) by the end of the century as per official statistics, mass poverty is the main problem.

In the circumstances the supreme consideration must be 'man' his economic and moral well-being. Poverty means lack of goods and services that go to satisfy man's necessities, basic. These goods and services are derived from agricultural and non-agricultural resource.

India is basically an agricultural country with a rural economy. The country is now producing more than enough foodgrains to feed the entire population, but agriculture in the country is still in crisis. Mr. Ramakrishna Bajaj, one of the leading industrialists in India recently says that rural regeneration through productive employment was the only way to resolve the paradox the country faced today – the pre-valence of wide-spread hunger despite the abundant availability of food. The co-existence of the two posed a serious challenge to the economic growth of the country. A solution to the problem of hunger and poverty lay in the execution of a well thought out and coordinated programme to raise the purchasing power of the rural people. According to the 1981 census more than 76 per cent of the total population (658 millions) is classified as 'rural', residing in 5.5 lakh villages. Nearly 70 per cent of this rural population derives their livelihood from agriculture directly or indirectly. According to one economist, while 91.4 millions of the main workforce of the country is cultivators, around 53.4 millions are farm labourers. The majority of farmers have very small landholdings which enable them to practice only subsistence farming. The uneconomic size of productivity, lack of resources and work opportunities and other inherent limitations have led to the breakdown of the rural economy.

How Mahatma Gandhi is Relevant Even Today?

It is precisely due to this miserable condition of rural India which has been living under the shadow of neglect and misery, the Gandhiji was adamant in stressing the human factor even decades back, in economic development. He could visualize the consequences this nation derived out of application of Western Technology.

Gandhiji always sought to build India from the bottom upwards, that is, from the poorest and weakest; hence followed the centrality of the village.

To the scientists of India, he said," I would like to be men, who stand up before the world firm in conviction. Let your zeal for the dumb millions be not stifled in the search for wealth." I tell you, he said," you can devise a far greater wireless instrument which does not require external research but internal and all research will be useless if it is not allied to internal research which can link your hearts with those of the millions. Unless all the discoveries that make the welfare of the poor as the end in view, all your workshops will be really no better than Satan's workshop. Hence if a temper of science has to flower we will have to begin with strengthening the weakest link in the economic chain of the land."

What Gandhiji envisages through his SARVODAYA is not against science and technology but he wants them to serve man and not control him. It is against destructive weapons of war and a technology that thrives on increasing the wants of the poor people without being able to satisfy them. Sarvodaya wants scientists to deal with problems that are relevant to the life around them; it needs a technology that is appropriate to the skills and resources that exist in society. It wants an optimum 'man-machine mix'.

That utilizes to the best advantage the creative energies of the vast number of people. It has no use for the machinery that throws people out of employment and services the few rich..

E.F. Schumacher, in his report to the Planning Commission in 1962, formulated the concept of an "intermediate technology", and said" it requires no lengthy argument to agree that India is 'long' in labour, 'short' in capital. This means that she requires a level of technology, or capital investment for workplace, which is likely to be very different from that current in western countries, which are long in capital and short in labour."

The evils of modern techniques emanate from two of its chief characteristics (1) its capital costs are very high and (2) it is applicable only in mass production. Therefore, the aim of new technology policy would be to select and develop techniques which can be employed by small producing groups and to make them available at a cost which they can afford.

Producation by Masses Vs Mass Product

We are not suggesting the blocking of scientific research or technological change altogether as some traditionalists would do. Advancement of science through new discoveries and inventions is a continuous process of natural evolution entwined with the progress of human civilization.

India has already gained the reputation that it is a repository of quite a large amount of modern technology and science. Still, apart from various other actors which put a strain on the effort of reform and improvement in the village scene, the fact that science has not been able to come to the rescue of the poverty-ridden rural populace is an important one.

The issue, therefore, is not technological improvement or no technological improvement. The issue is how much improvement? At what rate? Of what kind? What is required is the determination of the optimum rate of change of technique on the basis not only of the capital costs and the costs of production involved, but also a consideration of the employment effects and the other social and psychological repercussions of different techniques.

Nature, Human Values and Techniques

On human values, which are always held very high in Eastern countries, Mr. Raj Krishna says, "it is as erroneous to feel free where an iron logic operates as to feel helpless when there is scope for the exercise of free-will. The optimist's, notion that an Eastern country might important all the latest mass production techniques from the West and at the same time preserve vital values shows a lack of awareness of the logic of techniques." If these values are to be upheld, planning will have to readopt technology itself. It will have to include in its orbit, a rigorous selection, rejection and deliberate invention of techniques.

Under these circumstances, a new direction has to be sought for the use of science and technology, which should provide not only a lifeline to the weak and the down-trodden but pave a way for the world view to a future plan of human happiness; the basic requirements are a balanced relationship *(a)* between man and nature and *(b)* between individual interest and social interest. This unfortunately has not been kept in view, either by the scientists and technologists or by those who profit from them. The small industries catering to the needs of the local people utilizing the resources of nature in a way that maintain its balance, is being followed from ancient days. Gradually the industrial cities having a different code have changed the scene. Unless our knowledge of science is utilized fully to correct the situation, we are in for trouble.

In the new situation and general psychology developing in the country, it is necessary that due regard is given by the policy makers to the following points:

1. A greater commitment on the part of scientists and the scientific laboratories of the India for the eradication of the poverty of the land.
2. A national policy in which the requirements of the people living in mud huts will be given due priority.
3. That the social workers and enlightened people connected with the villages on the one hand the scientists working in the laboratories on the other will have a continuous communication so that they are able to understand the language of each other and to assist mutually in the crusade against poverty.
4. The Indian scientists may present, through their finding a technology suited to the villages, an alternative system which will give man a harmonious relationship with Mother Nature and brother man.

For this to take place, it is necessary that social workers who have had the privilege of identifying themselves with the problem of the man behind the mud-will and the talented scientists and technologists working to unravel my steries of nature for the benefit of humanity, get closer together to interpret each others language and try their best to take the fruits of scientific inventions to 'the last man'.

1. What are the proven technologies which could be recommended for promotion of rural based industries?
2. In which area (Production/manufacturing) additional capacity could reserved for rural sector.
3. What are the successful models of application or rural industrialization, based on modern S & T and in which areas these could be experimented?
4. When we talk of involvement of scientific community what is the mechanism and whether they need some incentive to get involved and committed?
5. Could consultancy services be set-up to support rural industrialization? If so, what should be their status, role and function?
6. What should be the guidelines for rural industrialization with consideration to avoid its adverse impact on established industries in se-urban and urban areas?
7. There are many risk factors involved in setting-up rural

based industries. Could risk insurance be provided for technology or for the total investment? What type of technology packages are needed to reduce risk of sickness and mortality of rural industry?

8. How to ensure that weaker sections of society including women are not neglected in the rural industrialization programme?
9. What facilities should be provided to voluntary agencies and business houses to promote latest technologies for rural industrialization (including horizontal transfer of technology)?
10. What modalities are to be adopted for technical manpower development for rural industrialization?
11. What are the priority areas keeping in view both technologies for mass production and those for production by masses?
12. What are the selective thrust areas for rural industrialization which require S & T answers including those traditional which need up gradation?

14

Gender Justice and Human Rights

Anil Dutta Mishra

Women are called fair sex but they always get unfair treatment. In fact a women's life lies between pleasure at one end and threat of violence at the other.

Women represent half the global population and one-third of the work force, they receive only one-tenth of the global income and less than one per cent of world property, and does two-thirds of all working hours. Still, day in and day out, our conscience is shocked by news of the violation of human rights.[1] The gender gap is increasing. This gender gap has tended to divide man and women into two different worlds, two separate planets, two unequal humanities. Today in high tech world women need freedom from – sexual exploitation, economic exploitation, rape, eve-teasing etc. She needs greater freedom in choosing career to life partner and from bed to corridor of power.[2]

The struggle to lift this curtain of unequal relationship and wipe out the unseen tear from the eyes of women are the most formidable challenge of our time. There are no easy answers, no quick-fix solutions to realize gender justice, which is the need of the hour.[3]

It is found that due to New Economic Policy (NEP) and the Structural Adjustment Programmes (SAP), women have been marginalised not only economically but politically and socially too. The process of Liberalisation, Privatisation and Globalisation have accentuated gender issues and catapulted Indian women on a crossroads. They cannot afford to follow the life style of western women as their cultural and social ethos has been different since the beginnings of history. Though the normative image of Indian women has undergone a sea change today due to multifarious factors, she is far from being identical with her western counterpart in her role expectations.

The impact of these policies on women, particularly in India, has been in some respects positive also. The pattern of women's participation in decision-making processes at all levels and in every sphere of life has dramatically changed in India. Undoubtedly, the welfare state in India is experiencing massive transformation in the era of new economic order which has a direct or indirect bearing on Gender justice and Human Rights.

Since ancient times women are facing problems. Their oppression is persistent and universal and its solutions are complicated. Many prophets of women's emancipation have come and gone, but discrimination against women and violation of human values persists.

Gender issue is basically one that affects women directly or indirectly. In other words, any social evil perpetrated at the cost of women, any law or custom that reinforces and institutionalises women's inferior status in society, or any event or series of events that affects large number of women can be regarded as a gender issue. Gender issues are also those that galvanise large numbers of women into action, any such issues, which catch the attention of women's groups, and subsequently of the media. There are a myriad other women's issues that are perenial, those that impinge on the life, health and work of women are women's issues.[4] There exists some ambiguity in interpreting the concept of gender, which is often confused with sex. While sex is biological determined, gender is socially determined on the basis of social and cultural patterns of behaviour in particular historical and social circumstances. Socially determined gender patterns impute values to the roles performed by men and women manifesting in gender bias or hierarchy between sexes.[5] Early socialization lays down rules about and provides role models for sex – appropriate behaviour and actions. Most societies have pattern of socialization, which encourage males and females to acquire differential attributes. Children are thus assigned a particular gender at birth and are indoctrinated to accept gender inequality as they grow.[6]

Gender justice is not a technocratic goal—it is a wholesale political commitment. Achieving it requires a long-term process in which all cultural, social, political and economic norms undergo fundamental change. It also requires an entirely new way of thinking—in which the stereotyping of women and men no longer limits their choices, but gives way to a new philosophy that regards all people as essential agents of change that view's development as a process of enlarging the choice of both sexes, just not one. Gender equality still eludes women in India where still access to healthcare services and education is marginally restricted.[7]

Gender justice means women must exercise full participation in decision-making process in all walks of life, and fully participation with men in all walks of life, and fully participating with men in finding equitable and practical solutions to issues in family and in society. Apart from this gender justice include women right to have control over and decide freely and responsibly on matters related to their sexuality, including sexual and reproductive health, free of coercion, discrimination and violence. Equal relationships between women and men in matters of sexual relations and reproduction including full respect for the integrity of the person, require mutual respect, consent and shared responsibility for sexual behaviour and its consequences.[8]

20th century has brought a great change in the life of women all over world and 21st century is the century of women. Women's attitudes, values, inspirations, ways of feelings, standards of behaviour and acting for effective participation in all walks of life. Rays of hope are becoming brighter and radical changes in and through women's thrust in socio-economic and political process, will be instrumental to healthier, happier and progressive state in near future. As the largest vibrant democracy in the world, India has been continuously experimenting with a number of forms and modes of organisations and structures to achieve gender equality. Even than gender bias and discrimination at every stage show, what kind of society women have to live in.

One can just think, the way the girls and boys grow up in their childhood. The reality of the Indian families is that, "boys are brought upto be served, girls to serve. Boys are princes in the family, girls maids in the scullery." In fact, women constantly suffer from discrimination in all fields of her life before and after coming on this earth. There is today clearly documented evidence to substantiate the claim that women are discriminated against and denied their fundamental right to survival, access to resources and control over their produce.

In recent years there has been an alarming increase of dowry deaths, sexual violence, and harassment of women, which reveals a large-scale societal breakdown. Women's position is worsening practically in every sphere, with the exception of some gains in education and employment for middle-class women. Women are still found in least- paid jobs, long working hours, and bearing full responsibility, for the home also by fetching fuel and water, by doing work in family production units, without being paid for labour, by bringing up children and looking after the sick and the aged. She does lots of thankless job silently.

This hour-to-hour and day-to-day contrast in the lives of men and women in our family and society, beginning from the childhood, creates a gender- bias, which through familiar, is patently unjust. The manifestation of gender violence may differ in different socio-economic and cultural settings but its impact, intensity and consequences on women remain the same. To understand the nature and forms of violence against women, one has to understand the function of violence as a maintenance mechanism of patriarchal society. The widespread gender violence is seen as both an indicator and means of perpetuating the low status of women, which also manifest itself through various not easily recognised forms of structural violence such as low health status, lack of access to higher education, employment and healthcare etc. In such a dismal scenario wherein women are generally powerless, direct violence against women appears to have the dual function of at once controlling women and perpetuating their subordinate status. And the physical violence aims at restricting women's physical mobility and to punish women who flout social norms in most society. All the public places are physically dominated by man, which means it is very difficult for women to move, work or earn living. When women defy this norm, it operates against them and affects all women, cutting across class barriers.

To unable women to fight against discrimination, it is necessary to empower them by ensuring their participation in decision-making bodies at all levels. These views are being expressed all over the world by women regardless of colour, religion or group as they are united in their fight for equality, social justice and democratic rights. India has been continuously experimenting with a number of forms and modes of organations and structures to achieve gender equality. No wonder, modernisation and westernisation have not really spelt liberation for the average women. Upliftment of women's status in India is today a searing issue that can only become a reality if suitable laws are passed and implemented strictly. Over the years, several laws have been amended and enacted for improving women's status and securing their basic rights. However, laws still exist that bluntly contradict all principles of gender justice and require change. The example that comes immediately to mind is the personal laws of different communities where several discriminatory provisions have been allowed to continue on one pretext or the other. Gender equality can be achieved if the law takes into consideration the special circumstances of women's life in which they are denied access to education, economic independence, etc.

Women's problems will be solved by women themselves. One primary goal of gender justice is the creation of a just, democratic and equal society. And for that women's empowerment is necessary and desirable. Here empowerment means that women need to be taken seriously. Equally important is enlightment of men, change their attitudes towards women and understand their problem.

Liberalisation, Privatisation and Globalisation have most adversely affected women collectively as well as individually, irrespective of their class, creed, economic status or their education level. It has most critically constructed the image of a "neo-women" – a very dangerous for it has led to a precarious transition in even the thought process of women of this generation. It has, in fact strengthened the set roles of women in the socio-economic cultural sphere from which she has to be freed to be accepted and treated as a human being. In fact women have already paid the heavy price due to LPG and SAP.

Women's human rights are violated in a variety of ways. Sometimes, of course, women suffer abuses (such as political repression) in ways that are much the same as those inflicted on men. But since the dominant image of the political actor in our world is male, the problem for women is visibility. Most women's experiences of human rights violations are gendered, and many forms of discrimination or abuse occur because the victim is female. Women whose rights are being violated for reasons other than gender (as political prisoners or members of persecuted ethnic groups) often also experience a particular form of abuse based on gender, such as sexual assault. [9]

Certain groups of women are particularly vulnerable to human rights violation. Women who come from marginalized groups are in double jeopardy. Discriminated against as women, they are also the victims of prejudice. [10] All over the world women are discriminated against in civil and criminal justice systems. In some countries, however, the law goes further; it does not only discriminate, it provides for particular cruel, inhuman and degrading punishments for offences committed by women. [11]

The majority of women who fall victim to human rights violations come from the poorest and most vulnerable groups in society; homeless women in the world's great cities, indigenous women, women belonging to socially disadvantaged groups such as the SCs and STs in india, ethnic minority women, women in immigrant communities, women who are criminalised because of their sexual orientation.

The great failure of the world community of government is not just that they have been unable to guarantee women their social, economic and cultural rights. Women's right to peace, development and equality are the prime issue in this high tech society world over. The growth of nationalist, secessionists and ethnic conflicts which threaten all regions of the world with violence and bloodshed has been armed opposition groups adopt similar methods of repression and terror in pursuit of their goals. Women have been killed, raped, and ill treated or taken hostage by armed opposition groups in all regions of the world. [12]

Women are in double jeopardy. Discriminated against as women, they are also as like men, if not more so, to become victims of human rights violations. Despite moves to introduce equality for women on the legislative and political front, discrimination on grounds of gender remains an international reality. Parliamentary Union Survey of 96 national parliaments, published in 1991, found that just 11 per cent of their numbers were women. While women are under-represented in national and international decision- making structures, they are over-represented among the victims of rights abuse. [13]

Discrimination is a deadly disease. More women and girl-children die each day from various forms at gender-based discrimination and violence than from any other type of human rights abuse. Every year, according to the UN Children's Fund (UNICEF), more than a million infant girls die because they are born female. Every year, because of discrimination, millions of women are mutilated, battered to death, burned alive, stripped of their legal rights, and bought and sold in an unacknowledged but international trade in slaves for domestic or sexual purposes. Because of their gender women are at risk of a range of violent abuses by private organizations and individuals.

The UN Declaration prohibiting gender violence calls for "the universal application to women of the rights and principles with regard to equality, security, liberty, integrity and dignity of all human persons." All the governments are morally obliged to uphold this Declaration. They are also bound by international human rights treaties not to violate the fundamental human rights of their citizens.

Women's rights are human rights and human rights are not only universal, they are also indivisible. A women who is arbitrarily detained, tortured, killed, made to "disappear" or jailed after an unfair trial has no chance of exercising her social, economic and cultural rights. Without respect for women's fundamental human rights—women's rights to peace, equality and development—are unattainable.

Even then no country in the world treats its women as well as men. Women from all social classes, cultures and races, in all societies, are at risk of abuse or their human rights. Discrimination in civil society can compound the risk to women's human rights. Often, discrimination against women is reflected in national law. If the law regards a woman as a second-class citizen, where is the incentive or the opportunity for society as a whole to respect women's human rights?

Human rights for women, as for all individuals, are protected in international law. Yet women suffer the full range of human rights violations known to the modern world. Women and girl- children also face human rights violations solely or primarily because of their sex.

The United Nation's Universal Declaration of Human Rights proclaims : "All Human beings are born free and equal in dignity and rights. "Yet women's freedom dignity, and equality are persistently compromised by law and by custom in ways that men's are not.

Women's rights must be understood as human rights. We must understand gender-based abuses as human rights abuses. Human rights must begin at home.

The only and most appropriate way to solve the problems of women is to change the position of the women in society and make her equally responsible for the well-being of the social order. This can be only achieved through fully implementing of Human Rights. Because human rights are women's rights.

'Basic Human Rights' Henery Kissinger said "must be presumed and cherished and defended if peace and prosperity are to be more than hollow technical achievements. Human rights are the very essence of a meaningful life, and human dignity is the ultimate purpose of government."

The international community particularly India and Canada can play a decisive role in protecting human rights through vigilant and concerted action. Important steps towards protecting women's human rights worldwide include documenting human rights violations, publicizing to press, government, and authorities for an end to the abuses.

The transformation of human rights from a feminist perspective is crucial to addressing global challenges to human rights in present day world.

The campaign to protect women's human rights will have to be waged on the same fronts and the same issues as that to protect everyone's human rights.

Conclusion

One may conclude by saying that women in India have to go a long way to attain the complete gender justice in political, economic, social and cultural field. The need of the hour are: not welfare, but development; not charity, but entitlement; not assistance, but empowerment; not structural adjustment, but structural change; not even social security but social and gender justice, if the women is to survive and flourish in the given situation.

REFERENCES

1. Anil Dutta Mishra, *Perspectives on Human Rights*, New Delhi, Radha Publications, 2002, p. 72.
2. *Ibid.*, p. 78.
3. *Ibid.*
4. Anil Dutta Mishra, "Communalism and Women" in Political Structures and Processes, Vol. 8, Centre for Women's Studies, Mysore, IDS, University of Mysore, p. 150.
5. Anjana Mangalagiri, " Gender and Role of Education in Structural Adjustment", in Education, Culture and Media, Vol. 2, Centre for Women's Studies, Mysore, IDS, University of Mysore, p.28.
6. *Ibid.*, p. 29.
7. Anil Dutta Mishra, No. 1, pp. 78-79.
8. *Ibid.*
9. Julie Peters and Andrea (Eds.), *Women's Rights Human Rights*, Routledge, 1995, p. 12.
10. Human Rights are Women's Right, Amnesty International, London, 1995, pp. 85-86.
11. *Ibid.*, p. 93.
12. *Ibid.*, pp. 4-5.
13. *Ibid.*

15

Human Development and Gender Issues: The Gandhian Perspective

Dr. G.A. Prabhakar and B. Siva Prasad

If you cannot change yourself, how can you change the world.

—Gandhi

Human Development is defined as a process of enlarging people's choices to lead a long and healthy life, to acquire knowledge and be educated, and to have access to resources needed for a decent level of living. Human Development is development of people, for the people and by the people: of the people means jobs and incomes, for the people means social services and by the people means participation.

Human Development is the most strategic and crucial determinant of economic growth. Paul Streeten argues a case for better education, nutrition and health is they help to raise labour productivity, enhance people's adaptability and capacity for change and create a suitable social and political environment for a stable government. He further pointed out that investment in sanitary facilities effects the health and health in turn influences education and these two in turn promote human capabilities, yield a return for the society.

Globalization is now considered as a factor of economic growth and it is also regarded as a pre-requisite for social progress. But growth by itself may not be enough to guarantee social progress; it must be sufficient condition for poverty reduction. The improvement of human well-being is related to economic growth. The growth of any economy influences human resource development. There is considerable evidence that the statistical correlation between GNP per capita and human development tends to work through the effect of higher GNP in raising public expenditure and in lowering poverty.

Human resource development is a multi-disciplinary concept, which includes the problem of health, food and nutrition, better housing, safe water supplies and sanitation that are required for improvement in the physical quality of life. The development of the quality of human beings as the production resources is one of the important strategies advocated for the economic development of less developed economies. Education and Health are the major components of economic development and they are also essential for improvements in the quality of life. Sen argued that in many places that liberalization would be beneficial provided land reforms, the provision of basic health and education facilities are under taken.

Development has no meaning if women who constitute 48 per cent of total population remain at the bottom. As pointed out by Amartya Sen illiteracy and gender inequality in India are two social failures leading to other failures. The two priorities envisaged in the Human Development Report 2003 are: *(i)* Ending Poverty, Ignorance and disease among masses of people and *(ii)* Ending inequality and making resources available to all, especially to the deprived masses.

The decade of the 1990s saw a visible shift in the focus of development planning from the mere expansion of the production of goods and services and the consequent growth of per capita income to planning for enhancement of human well - being. It is now realized that Human Development is about much more than the rise or fall of national incomes. It is about the quality of life, the level of human well-being and the access to basic social services.

The first Human Development Report (1990) brought out by the United Nations Development Programme (UNDP) started reminding us that the purpose of development is the flowering of Human Beings. Human Development centers focuses on the motion that Human Welfare depends on health and education in addition to GDP per capita. In conventional measures of economic output, health and educations contribution is measured essentially by the cost of producing the outcomes i.e., expenditure on schools and medical facilities.

The concept of Human Development was emphasized by Mahatma and he advocated the different dimensions with distinct style and values embedded.

Gandhiji's Approach to Economic Equality

Gandhiji considered economic equality as the master key to Non-Violence in independence. He believed that if we work for economic equality, eternal conflict between capital and labour would go. "It means the Leveling down of the few rich is stated in whose hands is concentrated the bulk of nation's wealth on the one hand, and the Leveling up of the semi-starved make millions on the other." He had the firm conviction that a non-violent to system of government was impossible as long as the wide Gulf between the rich and the hungry million persisted. He also believed that unless there was voluntary abdications of riches and resources were utilized for common good, the possibility of a violent and bloody revolution could not be ruled out.

"The Swaraj of my dream" declared Gandhiji, " is the Poorman's Swaraz." He believed that necessaries of life should be enjoyed by all in common and all persons irrespective of their work or profession, lawyers, doctors, teachers, sweepers, merchants and all others should get the same wages for an honest day's work.

Gandhiji's Approach to Women Empowerment

Status of Women and there Problems in the Society

Gandhi thoroughly studied the status of women in the past, the struggle they had undergone for the individuality, their place and their roles in the social structure. He evolved new methods for the social upliftment of women basing on the values of morality, equality and social justice. He integrated the old with the modern to bring out something new to uphold the women and their position in the society.

The Awakening of Women

Satyagraha has brought about the political awakening and quickened the pace of national life in other spheres also. Thus, women were largely emancipated from their bonds and could bear their due share in the national life. Women is considered to be the embodiment of sacrifice and suffering. The practice of non-violence involves the avoidance of the suppression of women. Women has as much right as man in the matter of shaping her own destiny in a plan of life based on non-violence. Gandhi was more concerned for the welfare of women. He stated that the largest part of the human effort for promoting the regeneration of women should be directed towards removing the blemishes represented in the shastras as necessary requisite ingrained in the characteristics of women. He held that it is the privilege of the awakened women to spot out the age-long evils and eradicate them.

Women and Education

In the year 1936 Gandhi raised the question about the boys and girls who completed their courses is their courses in the colleges but they were unable or unwilling to resist the evil manifested in custom of compulsory marriage with dowry which effects their future. Gandhi stood for proper education for women and believed that in proportion to the education they receive, they would become sensitive to the glaring inequalities, which they are subject to. The absence of education for women is felt to be responsible for then low status is the society. Gandhi pointed out that there was no justification for men to deprive or deny women of their equal rights on the ground of their illiteracy.

Gandhi State

"Education is essential for enabling women to assert these natural rights to exercise them wisely, and to walk for their expansion again true knowledge in unattainable by the millions who lack such education."

Women and Legal Equality

Gandhi held that woman should labour under no legal disability not suffered by man. He should treat the daughter and son on the same footing of perfect equality. The education that has been imparted a woman helps to realize her strength and she would naturally resent to glaring inequality to which she is subjected to. Gandhi was of the opinion that mere removal of in legal inequalities would remain a mere palliative. He found that they root of the evil lies much deeper than must of the people could realize. The Indian national congress, which was guided by Gandhi, had always walked for raising the status of women and to impure has social conditions.

Gandhi was aware of the various social customs observed by women and their state of mind. He stood against the evil social practices viz., child marriages, the deplorable living conditions of women is the society, the practices of Sati, and the possessions of more than one wife by a single man and numerous other obnoxious customs which were to be tackled. Gandhi wished to seek public opinion in these matters.

Women and Social Justice

Gandhi recognized clearly that woman has a vital role to play is the matter of the reconstruction of the society. He fought for this woman's rights in order to bring about social justice to realize equality. He held that woman should have same liberty and opportunity for self-development as man. Gandhi said – "I make no distinction between man and woman. Woman should feel just as independent as man. Bravery is not man's monopoly."

Women and their Role in Society

Gandhi opined that man and woman are equal and then problems must be one and the same in essence. Since both name the same feelings, both are complementary to each other. Both are independent and they cannot live without the others active life.

In his address on 20th February, 1918, Gandhi dealt in detail with the problems faced by woman and their regeneration.

He Stated That

Woman is the companion of man, gifted with equal mental capabilities. She has the right to participate in every minutest detail in the activating man and she has an equal right of freedom and liberty with him. She is entitled to a supreme place in her own sphere of activity as man is in his. This ought to be the natural condition of things and not as a result only of learning to read and write.

Gandhiji's "Approach to Sanitation"

Gandhiji's interest in Sanitation was largely linked to his concern about the untouchables who performed the unclean task of handling excrete and cleaning of latrines and were treated with disdain and indignities. Gandhiji said assumptions of superiority by any person over any other are a sin against God and Man. In the Ashrams that Gandhi established for pursuing his work, he cleaned his own latrine as others living in Ashram also did.

Conclusion

Gandhiji practiced what he preached. If he was concerned about the 'poorest of the poor' he adopted a life style, which reflected his constituency. When the textile labour in Ahmedabad went on strike under Gandhi's leadership and complained of hunger and starvation, Gandhi himself went on a fast. And if he preached cleanliness and upliftment of Harijans he himself undertook the 'scavengers' work and emphasized the importance of inner and outer cleanliness. Millions of people followed him. He emphasized that we must change ourselves before we can change others, which our real enemies are within.

We can say proudly Gandhi's views on various indicators of human development are in vogue now all economies, which Gandhi mentioned a century ago. All his ideas reflects a healthy image of a nations development. Hence, it is necessary for the worlds economies to practice his philosophy of human development for better society.

REFERENCES

Prabhat Patnaik (1998), "Amartya Sen and the Theory of Public Action" *Economic and Political Weekly*, Vol.XXIII, No. 45, Nov. 7-13, 1998.

Paul Streeten and Others (1981), *First Things First: Meeting Basic Human Needs in the Developing Countries*, Oxford University Press, Newyork.

Human Development Report, 2003.

Mohandas Karamchand Gandhi, *Hind Swaraj and Other Writings* (Cambridge: Cambridge University Press, 1997).

Gandhi, M.K. (1958), "All Man are Brothers", ed. Krishna Hripalni , New York, Columbia, p. 76.

Harijan, August 26, 1936.

Vivek Pinto 1998, "Gandhi is Vision a Values—the Moral Quest for Change in Indian Agriculture" Sage Publications, New Delhi.

16
Trusteeship

D.K. Oza

I am happy that a very important aspect of Gandhian philosophy namely Trusteeship is the focus of this seminar. This important subject is not being discussed very often either in printed literature or in seminars, symposia etc.

Generally speaking Mahatma Gandhi raised important issues rather briefly. Very often, he did not elaborate them or work out completely the details. He wrote so much, spoke so much, and communicated so much that his views on various important subjects have to be often compiled from his speeches and writings over a long period of time. This understanding about how his mind worked is basic to a full appreciation. I will give only two examples of this. He wrote his classic "Autobiography, My Experiments with Truth", in a serial form in Gujarati language in his weekly Harijan Sewak. Similarly his fine Book "History of Satyagraha in South Africa" was written serially. Both were eventually published in book form. Since Mahatma Gandhi was basically a journalist from his Journal "Indian Opinion" in South Africa, right up to his passing away in 1948, he gave his views in those journals. He replied to letters with exemplary punctuality and the more important letters he received – and the replies he sent – were published for the larger public. It was for others to be alert and keep checking what he wrote, where he wrote it and when and why. That is why the compilations of his views by scholars are very important. I think the best among them is "India of My Dreams." Others like "To the Students", "Trusteeship", "Khadi", "To Women" etc., are also very important to understand what the Mahatma wrote at different times.

The only booklet he ever wrote as a single piece is "The Constructive Programme—its meaning and place" and "Anasakthiyoga" which is his very brief commentary on the Bhagavad Gita.

Now on the main point regarding Trusteeship—Mahatma Gandhi held the belief that everything which any individual is really a Trust in his custody and in that sense, he or she is a Trustee. It is true that he was specifically referring to the Trusteeship of wealth by owners of industry, land etc. But he meant everything really: your learning. Your talent etc. I think in modern terms, we will have to discover ways of how to apply this principle to the modern situation. Part of the answer is that the principle of "Corporate Social Responsibility"(CSR) will have to be clearly understood. I believe that some industrial houses and businesses accept the need that they have to devote part of their profit and wealth to the service of the entire community. I must say that some very famous groups in India have done remarkable contributions to advancement of science, education, health and social welfare by devoting substantial amounts and efforts of discharging their Corporate Social Responsibility. Let us hope that more and more wealthy industries and individuals do this.

There is another way of ensuring that the requirements of CSR are fulfilled. That is called "Social Audit." As everyone knows every business has to fulfill the legal requirements of financial audit; that has to be submitted to the Government authorities. In addition, some institutions do "performance audit" and some do the "Swot Analysis" (strength and weakness, opportunities and threats). What is now missing is the "social audit" which I think could be undertaken by a group of enlightened citizens. The social audit will contain two separate sections—Negative and Positive. The negative portion will ask questions like—Has this Industry caused any harm to the environment or polluted the earth/water?The positive analysis will ask—has this Industry organized social service and philanthropic activities to benefit the larger community?

This kind of Social Audit can best be undertaken by a group which would include Gandhians. I consider this very important because under the new liberal industrial policy, we will have big business houses with a turn over of millions of rupees without a set of guidelines and yet which affect large numbers of people and geographical areas. Also the entry of multinationals makes such Social Audit very important. All this must be undertaken in the Gandhian spirit and Gandhian methods. What I mean is that it should not be undertaken in a spirit of just finding fault, but must aim at sustained improvement.

There could be other ways of enhancing the the "Trusteeship" principle given by Mahatma Gandh, and these methods could be discovered only through a sustained debate.

17

Gandhiji's Alternative Economic Systems: Trusteeship

P.V.V.S.N. Raju and D.L. Deepak

On the Economic Front, particularly in respect of property relations, Gandhiji opposed both the moderate corporate culture of capitalistic countries and the bureaucratic statism of communist countries. In both cases, the worker is alienated as he has not much say with the collective self-worship of the decision-making machine.

The corporate system has undergone considerable changes in decision-making from ownership to management and at lower levels, workers may have been given freedom to participate, but the personality of the corporation and the personality of the individual stand poles apart. All the experiments that have been done to widen the ownership of shares or introduce some king of workers management have only touched the fringe of the problem.

On the other hand, the growing power and privileges of the communist party and the government bureaucracy have negated the Marxian concept of a man and produced its own counter-revolution. In this connection, Gandhiji produced a grand alternative i.e., the Trusteeship. However, Trusteeship is a much misunderstood concept. Both the communists and capitalists seem to consider it some kind of an Umbrella under which the existing system can justify itself in a modified forms. It is our failure that we have not filled the gap between image and reality.

Marx favoured collective ownership of all instruments of production as a remedy for the inequity of the capitalist system. But Gandhiji believed that restructuring of institutions would be of no avail unless the men who operate these institutions accept; of their own volition, the implicit ethics of the new systems and evolved the concept of Trusteeship.

Trusteeship Formula

1. Trusteeship provides a means of Transforming the present capitalist order of society into an egalitarian one. It gives no quarter to capitalism, but gives the present owning class, a chance of reforming itself. It is based on the faith that human nature is never beyond redemption.
2. It does not recognize any right of private ownership of property except so far as it may be permitted by society for its own welfare.
3. It does not exclude legislative regulation of the ownership and use of wealth.
4. Thus, under state-regulated trusteeship, an individual will not be free to hold or use his wealth for selfish satisfaction or in disregard of the interest of society.
5. Just as it is proposed to fix a decent minimum living wage, even so a limit should be fixed for the maximum income that could be allowed to any person in society. The difference between such minimum and maximum incomes should be reasonable and equitable and variable from time-to-time so much so that the tendency would be towards obliteration of the difference.
6. Under this economic order, the character of production will be determined by social necessity and not by personal whim or greed.

Analysis of the Concept of Trusteeship

There are three important aspects of Trusteeship which correspond to the Gandhian values. Firstly, it demands transfer of ownership from individual either directly or via the state. Also form the state to common ownership among those who would run an enterprise. Those who would consume its products and those who will represent larger against sectional interests, with all the built-in provisions of social priorities.

Secondly, Trusteeship is not a limited economic exercise, it is a non-violent movement or method of dispossessing the owners of wealth and property. The details of which have been given Gandhiji himself, but in actual practice, they have to be worked out in each different situation.

Thirdly, the Trusteeship will have to satisfy conditions of ethical economics i.e., create those conditions of production and consumption economics which do not permit greed, conflict or alienation among different classes of the society including the worker.

The ethical norms which emanate from the Gandian philosophy would remain the guiding principles of these organizations.

Trusteeship – Operational Feasibility

One of the major mis-conceptions of the Trusteeship is that it is an utopian in nature and practically cannot be implemented. But, many if the Tribal Communities of Northeast India, without being aware of it, are actually following practices which are very close to Gandhiji's concept of Trusteeship. In the bulk of the tribal areas of Northeast India, the land and land-based resources are traditionally held by specific communities. The headmen or Clan Elders serve only as custodians. There are attempts on the part of the administrative to persuade the custodians to claim ownership rights over the resources, so that by Clandestine arrangements with them the resources can be taken over for capitalist market-oriented bureaucratic or corporate management systems. There are however cases, where the concerned headmen have resisted the temptation. There are also cases whereby managing their resources, the communities have created social infrastructures, institutional networks and even production infrastructures.

Further, Gandhiji himself, in an article wrote to the newspaper 'HARIJAN' dated 16th December, 1939 expressed confidence in the Trusteeship theory by stating that " My Theory of Trusteeship is no make-shift certainly no camouflage, I am confident that it will survive all other theories. It has the sanction of philosophy and religion behind it."

Relevancy of the Concept in the Era of Globalisation

If one carefully observes the developments in social, economic, political and cultural domains during the last two decades, one gets a clear message, Dominence and Hegemony of market forces in social domains and weakening of social and cultural bonds as a result of globalisation.

Further, other unhealthy practices such as increasing number of lock outs and Industrial closures, Massive retrenchment of the staff, Take-overs of Industrial units by the MNC's and voluntarily (if not compulsorily) retiring of old-hands, weakening and diluting the labour laws to break the labour unions and their solidarity etc., can also be attributed to the impact of globalisation. Therefore, the remedy for the above evils may be found in the Trusteeship concept and hence this concept is still more relevant even in the New Millennium.

18
Gandhiji's Vision and Values

Alan Nazareth

Gandhi's vision, though considered utopian by some and arcadian by others, was actually an elevated, wide spectrum, deeply spiritual yet practical one. Like the tall redwood tree, which views the farthermost horizon, yet is fully aware of every environmental nuance around its sumptuous girth and at its deepest root, Gandhi perceived the macro and micro effects of human behaviour in diverse fields. His vision can justifiably therefore be described as extraordinary.

The prime component of Gandhi's vision was his firm conviction that humans, the highest manifestation of God's creation, can and would live in harmony and peace, firmly adhering to Truth, Justice, Love and Non-Violence. "Non-violence is the law of our species as violence is the law of the brute. The spirit lies dormant in the brute and he knows no law but that of physical might. The dignity of man requires obedience to a higher law – that of the spirit.... It is the law of love that rules mankind. Had violence i.e. hate ruled us, we should have become extinct long ago. Mankind has to get out of violence only through non-violence. Hatred can be overcome only by love."

In his historical perspective he saw dictators and tyrants maintaining their fearful sway only temporarily. All empires built with the sword end up in the dustbin of history; only those built on the spirit with truth, love and self-sacrifice by the great seers and prophets have survived and flourished. Since humans are created "in the image of God" and are imbued with the "Divine Spark" they have to be led by truth and love, not by fear and hate. One has to live, and if necessary to die for truth, but never to hurt or kill anyone.

For Gandhi, Truth (*Satya*) was as real and omnipotent as God himself. In fact, Truth is God, as Truth is what is and God is the only reality that always is. "The world rests upon the bedrock of Satya ... which being what is can never be destroyed. This is the doctrine of Satyagraha in a nutshell." Truth is the 'Right Path' and it is 'Right that is Might' not its opposite. He often quoted the Bhagavad Gita's core philosophical assertion 'Satyanasti paro Dharma' (There is no greater duty than adherence to Truth). Truth implies Justice and both are essential requisites for the attainment of peace. "Peace will come when Truth is pursued, and Truth implies Justice." Justice requires that the adversary's views and requirements be given due consideration. "Three-fourths of the miseries and misunderstandings in the world would disappear if we step into the shoes of our adversaries and understand their standpoint." Justice also requires that the final agreement made be acceptable to all concerned.

Whereas Gandhi was passionately dedicated to Truth even as a youth, particularly after he learnt about Harish Chandra's unshakable adherence to it despite innumerable hardships, his deep commitment to non-violence came only in his early thirties after he read Christ's 'Sermon on the Mount' and Tolstoy's 'The Kingdom of God is Within You'. The strong non-violence traditions of the Jain community of his native Gujarat had of course mentally prepared him for this. Non-violence thus became his immutable path for realization of Truth. For him, it meant complete abstention not only from all physical, mental and emotional injury to others but also cleansing oneself of all hatred and desire for revenge. One had to hate and confront evil but nonetheless love the evil doer because even he is endowed with the Divine spark which love can ignite and induce his conversion . "Non-violence is based on the assumption that human nature in its essence is one and therefore unfailingly responds to the advances of love...The hardest metal yields to sufficient heat. Even so, the hardest heart must melt before the heat of non-violence and there is no limit to the capacity of non-violence to generate heat."

For him: "The objective of all non-violent activity is always a mutually acceptable agreement, never the defeat, much less the humiliation of the opponent" and "A non-violent revolution is not a programme for seizure of power. It is a programme for transformation of relationships ending in a peaceful transfer of power."

Next to truth, justice, love and non-violence courage, compassion, determination and dedication were high among Gandhi's values. He was not born courageous. In his childhood and youth he was extremely timid and was greatly afraid of snakes, ghosts, thieves and darkness. It was his devoted maid Rambha who enabled him to overcome these fears by persuading him that invoking the name of Lord Ram was an effective antidote for all fears. At school he was an active participant in various activities, including sports, and at times even functioned as an umpire. But this self-confidence was only among those he was very familiar with. When, on his return from London, he commenced legal practice in Bombay in 1893, he was still so timid he failed to argue his first brief. In his autobiography he writes, " I stood up, but my heart sank into my boots..My head was reeling and I felt as though the whole court was doing likewise. I could think of no question to ask. The judge must have laughed, but I was past seeing anything. I sat down and told the client that I could not conduct the case. I hastened from the court not knowing whether my client won or lost her case. I was ashamed of myself and decided not to take up any more cases until I had courage enough to conduct them. Indeed I did not go to court again until I went to South Africa."

His transformational change came within ten days of his arrival in South Africa. He was on his way from Durban to Johannesberg when he was thrown out of the train at Pietermaritzberg he had a valid first class ticket, was well dressed and had inconvenienced no one. His crime was being seated in a "whites only" compartment and refusing to shift to the "van". He was just 24 years old then. In his autobiography he writes "I began to think of my duty. Should I fight for my rights or go back to India.... It would be cowardice to run back to India without fulfilling my obligation. The hardship to which I was subjected was superficial—only a symptom of the deep disease of colour prejudice. I should try if possible to root out the disease and suffer the hardships in the process." Many years later, when questioned by Christian missionary John Mott as to what was the most "creative experience" of his life, he replied that it was the Pietermaritzberg episode. "That changed the course of my life. My active non-violence began from that date and God put me through the test during that very journey." However, the enunciation of his doctrine of Satyagraha was still thirteen years away.

The key to understanding Gandhi's transformation from extreme timidity to fearless leadership is to be found in the evolution of his spiritual make-up. He had been brought up as a devout Vaishnava Hindu and remained a lifelong devotee of Lord Ram. However, he had not read the Bhagawad Gita until he got to London, where he learnt about it from two Theosophists who had become acquainted with it through Edwin Arnold's 'Song Celestial'. Subsequently he read and memorized the Gita in its Gujarati and Sanskrit versions. It became his "infallible guide of conduct", his "dictionary of daily reference" and "the book par excellence for the knowledge of Truth" It taught him the vital truths that the soul is immortal, that death is not an end but a new beginning, and that when confronted with untruth and injustice, one's bounden duty was to confront it. His first acquaintance with the Bible and Christ's 'Sermon on the Mount' was also in London. The latter became a vital input in his adoption of non-violence as the other pillar of his Truth based Satyagraha strategy.

'Satyagraha' was born soon after the historic September 11, 1906 mass meeting at the Imperial Theatre in Johannesberg, which Gandhi had convened and at which, according to Louis Fischer, he showed "awesome, Himalayan self-assurance." Following the collective vow participants at this meeting took, he offered a prize for an appropriate name for the new non-violent struggle they had decided upon. A cousin, Maganlal Gandhi suggested "Satyagraha" (firmness in a good cause). Gandhi amended it to "Satyagraha" (firm adherence to Truth). Louis Fischer annotates it thus "For Gandhi, Satyagraha was "the vindication of Truth not by infliction of suffering on the opponent but on one's self." That requires self control. The weapons of the Satyagrahi are within him. Satyagraha is peaceful. If words fail to convince the adversary perhaps purity, humility and honesty will. The opponent must be "weaned from error by patience and sympathy", weaned not crushed, converted not annihilated... "You cannot inject new ideas into a man's head by chopping it off; neither will you infuse a new spirit into his heart by piercing it with a dagger."

In 1918, twenty-five years after the Pietermaritzberg episode, he wrote "We are regarded as a cowardly people" and recommended Satyagraha as a technique to transform Indians, just as it had transformed him, from extreme timidity to fearlessness.

For him non-violence is "the weapon of the really brave" and "He who fears, fails." As the armour of the non-violent warrior is his unshakable faith in God, he has, nothing to fear not even death for even death can be victory. "They may torture my body, break my bones, even kill me but then they will have my dead body, not my obedience." Among his other notable affirmations on fearlessness are: "Fear and Truth are mutually contradictory terms"; "Being a slave to fear is the worst form of slavery"; "The golden rule is to act fearlessly upon what one believes to be right"; "The greatest help you can give me is to banish fear from your hearts"; "You do not know what a coward I was when I was young. I am not quite a coward today. Multiply my example and you will have one whole nation shaking off its cowardice"; "It is any day better to stand erect with a broken and bandaged head than to crawl on one's belly in order to save one's head"; "Strength does not come from physical capacity. It comes from an indomitable will."

Gandhi's compassion is clearly seen in his constant focus on the oppressed and impoverished. He identified himself and empathized with them, dressed like them and after 1917 even lived like them in a mud hut, though brought up in comparitive luxury in his youth and held a British legal degree. "I shall work for an India in which the poorest shall feel that it is their country, in whose making they have an effective voice," he affirmed.

In his long letter to the Viceroy Lord Irwin prior to the Salt March he wrote, "Why do I regard the British rule as a curse? Because it has impoverished the dumb millions by a system of progressive exploitation and by a ruinous, expensive military and civil administration which the country cannot afford." References to the "impoverished dumb millions" were numerous and frequent in his speeches and writings. His emphasis on Khadi was primarily for their benefit. "Khadi means employment for the poor and freedom for India. Britain holds India because it is a fine market for Lancashire...."

His compassion is also testified by the "talisman" he gave to India's nationalists "Whenever you are in doubt, try the following expedient. Recall the face of the poorest and the most helpless man whom you have seen and ask yourself whether the step you contemplate is going to be of any use to him. Will he be able to gain anything by it? Will it restore to him control over his own life and destiny? In other words, will it lead to self rule for the hungry and spiritually starved millions of our countrymen?"

However, the best testimony of his compassion is his walking barefoot on his visit to Naahkali in August, 1947. When his grand daughter Manu protested he replied, "We do not go to our temples, mosques or churches with shoes on... We now tread on that holy ground where people have lost their loved ones... How can I wear chappals there?"

Gandhi's dedication, particularly to India's unity and prevention of its partition is testified by his fourteen meetings with Jinnah in September 1944 during which he even offered him the Prime Minister's office but to no avail. He humbled himself to go to Jinnah's residence at 10 Mount Pleasant Road, Mumbai for all these fourteen meetings even though his domestic and international stature was higher than Jinnah's.

When Gandhi was assassinated in January 1948 his only earthly possessions were two sets of wrap around cotton cloths, a wrist watch, his spectacles, three sacred books, two wooden food bowls and spoons, two pairs of wooden sandals and a walking stick! This is dedication and self-abnegation par excellence.

The firmness of Gandhi's determination is seen in his promptly calling off his March 1919 Satyagraha when incidents of violence occurred. In calling it off he declared "I had called on the people to launch upon civil disobedience before they had qualified themselves for it and this mistake seemed to me of Himalayan magnitude". Commenting on this Vincent Sheean wrote "No act of his life was more bewildering to the Indian masses than Gandhi's abandonment of Gandhi's possessions Satyagraha at this moment. It took a long time for Indians in general, Hindus as well as Moslems, to understand that the frail little man meant what he said, that he had a will of iron, and that no power on earth could induce him to pursue an action if he felt that it violated his principles."

His determination is also seen in his historic "fast unto death" in September 1932 over the British grant of a separate electorate for "untouchables." He saw this as a nefarious device to split the Hindu fold and perpetuate untouchability. He gave up the fast only when Dr. B.R. Ambedkar, the untouchable leader, agreed he would accept

Gandhi's assurances of equitable treatment for his community and not avail of the separate electorate. The Poona Pact of September 25, 1932, embodied these assurances and is a good indication of Gandhi's "victory for both sides" approach. In return for giving up the separate electorate, Ambedkar secured an increase of "untouchable" reserved seats from the 71 the British had offered, to 149! About the Poona Pact Rajmohan Gandhi writes, "From behind bars, a prisoner had jolted a nation's customs and imposed his will on an empire...The world seemed to marvel and a writer in the Boston Globe said that the debt Gandhi undertakes to settle is the debt of the human conscience to other human consciences."

Gandhi's compassion, dedication and determination are all embodied in his visit to Calcutta to stem the communal killings there rather than be in New Delhi to participate in the Independence Day celebrations in New Delhi on August 15th, 1947. "The interior voice tells me to go on fighting against the whole world, even though I am alone." James K. Mathews commends Gandhi's determination thus "In great part his secret of leadership was in his strength of purpose. He was ever and ever restating it so that it might be clear to himself and to his associates."

Manganimity, self-assurance, composure and good humour were also characteristic of Gandhi. His magnanimity is best seen in his forgiveness of those who hated, reviled and attacked him. On four separate occasions he was attacked—in Durban in January 1897, in Johannesberg in January 1908, in Pune in June 1933 and in New Delhi on January 22, 1948 (when a bomb exploded at his prayer meeting). In every case he forgave his attackers and insisted they should not be prosecuted. His statement after the arrest of the Pathans involved in the Johannesberg attack, was typical; "They should be released. They thought they were doing what was right and I have no desire to prosecute them."

Among his greatest political revilers were Ambedkar, Churchill and Jinnah. The former castigated him as "the most dishonest politician in Indian history...with pernicious saintly idiosyncracies"; the latter contemptuously described him a "a half naked and seditious fakir" and "an old humbug." Yet Gandhi spoke of them thus :

> " I have the highest regard for Dr. Ambedkar. He has every right to be bitter. That he does not break our heads is an act

of self restraint on his part.....The same thing happened to me in my early days in South Africa where I was hounded out by the Europeans wherever I went. It is quite natural for him to vent his wrath."

"Mr. Churchill is a great man. He belongs to the blue blood of England. The Marlborough family is very famous in British history. He took the helm when Great Britain was in great danger and saved the British Empire from a great danger at that time."

Meeting the press after the breakdown of his 14 long sessions of talks with Jinnah in 1944 he said, "We have parted as friends. These days have not been wasted. I am convinced that Mr. Jinnah is a good man. I hope we shall meet again. I am a man of prayer and I shall pray for understanding."

Gandhi was well-endowed with self-assurance, composure and humour. When, after the 2nd Round Table Gandhi was received by King George V., the latter curtly asked "Why did you boycott my son?" (referring to the Gandhi instigated boycott of the 1921 Prince of Wales' India visit). Gandhi promptly responded "Not of your son, Your Majesty, but of the official representative of the British Crown." When leaving Buckingham Palace, journalists expressed surprise at his calling on the King dressed the way he was. He nonchalantly replied " His Majesty was dressed enough for both of us! " Pearl Buck commended Gandhi's humour thus "Gandhi was not only a saint; he was a humorist. The two are not often in combination, but when they are the creature is invincible."

Gandhi's patriotism and nationalism were broad visioned, in keeping with the ancient Indian maxim *Udara charita nam tu vasudaiva Kudumbakam* (for the broad minded all mankind is one family). He did not regard India as a nation in the narrow sense;it was a civilization with special spiritual qualities and a duty to serve humanity. "I live for India's freedom and would die for it. But my patriotism is not exclusive. It is calculated to benefit all in the true sense of the word. Through the deliverance of India, I seek to deliver the so-called weaker races of the world.... For me, patriotism is the same as humanity. It is not exclusive. I am patriotic because I am human and humane. I will not hurt England or Germany to serve India." On nationalism he wrote: "My nationalism includes the love of all nations of the earth irrespective of creed ....It is not nationalism that is evil; it is the narrowness, selfishness, exclusiveness which is the bane of modern nations which is evil. Indian nationalism has, I hope, struck a different path to find full self-expression for the benefit and service of humanity at large."

Gandhi's enlightened nationalism is also seen in his attitude to religions other than his own. Though a deeply devout Hindu, his approach was "sarvadharma samabhav" (equal respect for all religions) and a "spiritualized humanism". All religions had equal status and were different paths to the same goal of achieving union with the Divine. His religion was that "which transcends Hinduism, which changes one's very nature, binds one indissolubly to the truth within and ever purifies. It is the permanent element in human nature which leaves the soul restless until it has found itself." He affirmed "For me different religions are beautiful flowers from the same garden or branches of the same majestic tree." He often said he was as much a Moslem, Christian, Sikh, Buddhist, Jain and Parsee as he was Hindu and added "The hands that serve are holier than the lips that pray." At his prayer meetings there were readings from all the holy books. His favourite hymn began with the line "He alone is a true devotee of God who understands the pains and sufferings of others."

Gandhi's fundamental contribution in the field of religion was to give primacy to Truth rather than conformity to traditional practices. In fact he made Truth the basis of all morality by declaring: "I reject any religious doctrine that does not appeal to reason and is in conflict with morality.....God did not create men with the badge of superiority or inferiority; no scripture which labels a human being an inferior or untouchable because of his or her birth can command our allegiance. It is denial of God and Truth which is God." He affirmed, "Independent India as conceived by me will have all Indians belonging to different religions, living in perfect friendship." In 1931, he wrote in Young India "It has been said that Swaraj will be the rule of the majority community i.e. the Hindus....If this were to be true, I for one would refuse to call it Swaraj and would fight it with all the strength at my command. For to me Hind Swaraj is the rule of all the people and the rule of justice." Lauding this enlightened approach Fischer wrote "Mahatma Gandhi, a supremely devout Hindu, was incapable of discriminating against anyone on account of religion, race, caste, colour or anything. His contribution to the equality of untouchables and to the education of a new generation which was Indian instead of Hindu or Moslem or Parsee or Christian has world significance."

On the eve of the San Francisco Conference which created the United Nations, Gandhi issued a statement with the following paragraph in it: "I reiterate my conviction that there will be no peace for the allies or the world unless they shed their belief in the efficacy of war and its accompanying terrible deception and fraud. Peace must be just... The fruits of peace must be equally shared. Exploitation and domination of one nation over another can have no place in a world striving to put an end to all wars.

In March 1947, in his address to the closing session of the Asian Relations Conference at New Delhi he said, "It will be a sorry thing if we go away from this conference without a firm determination that Asia shall live and live as free as every Western nation.... If you want to give a message to the West it must be the message of love and the message of truth."

That is the message which India, Asia and the world needs today as much as the West. That is also the ideal path for achieving personal and spiritual development as Gandhiji so convincingly demonstrated in his own life and his 'Experiments with Truth'.

19

Constructive Programme and Its Relevance Today

G.V.V.S.D.S. Prasad

During the Freedom Struggle, Mahatma Gandhi provided the Nation with the Constructive Programme which contained 18 aspects of work. While he offered Satyagraha against British imperialism, the Constructive Programme is to provide consciousness through training. Constructive programme is the truthful and non-violent way of winning Poorna Swaraj. Its wholesale fulfillment is complete Independence.

Satyagraha is the policy of non-violent resistance initiated in India by Mahatma Gandhi as a means of pressing for political reform. Gandhiji called his overall method of non-violent action Satyagraha. This translates roughly as "Truth-force." A fuller rendering, though, would be "the force that is generated through adherence to Truth. Civil Disobedience, mass or individual, is an aid to constructive effort and is a full substitute for armed revolt. Training is necessary as well for civil disobedience as for armed revolt. Only the ways are different. Action in either case takes place only when occasion demands.

Training for military revolt means learning the use of arms ending perhaps in the atomic bomb. For civil disobedience it means the Constructive Programme. Gandhiji said, "For my handling of Civil Disobedience without the constructive programme will be like a paralysed hand attempting to lift a spoon."

Satyagraha and Constructive Programme are like the two wheels of a cart. Both are important and inseparable. While Satyagraha can be considered as a direct action against injustice, Constructive

Programme is a peace time activity. This is what prepares Satyagrahis through constant training and attachment. It is a regular reminder of the commitment of an individual.

Constructive Progrmme is a means for attainment of Poorna Swaraj. Here, Swaraj connotes a wider meaning than mere independence. Swaraj is self-rule, self-control and self-respect. It reminds one of one's duties and of good conduct. Swaraj has no meaning in the absence of training of citizen. Constructive programme imparts that orientation.

Constructive Programme deals with the areas of activities which are essential to building our society. It has economic programmes, social programmes and national programmes. It is not all inclusive and can always be expanded depending upon the circumstances. All Patriots, Sarvodaya Karyakarthas should adopt and practice some of the components of Constructive Programme.

The following are the activities included in the Constructive Programme:

1. Communal Unity
2. Removal of Untouchabilty
3. Prohibition
4. Khadi
5. Other Village Industries
6. Village Sanitation
7. New or Basic Education
8. Adult Education
9. Women
10. Education in Health and Hygiene
11. Provincial Languages
12. National Language
13. Economic Equality
14. Kisans (Farmers)
15. Labour
16. *Adivasis* (Tribals)
17. Lepers
18. Students.

20

Enduring Significance of the First Satyagraha

S.N. Sahu

Peoples across the world are familiar with the term 9/11. It became notoriously famous for the savage terrorist attack on the United States of America and was interpreted as one of the worst and deadliest attacks on freedom, democracy and civilized existence. The very reference to the term 9/11 sends shock waves through the spines of the peoples of the globe who are now confronting the menace of terrorism never before witnessed in any period of human history. In fact the present age, described as the age of fear due to the upsurge of fanaticism and terrorism, is going to last for quite some time causing pain and misery to citizens and constantly haunting them of that terrible event. The paranoia spread by the very mention of 9/11 is symbolic of the problems associated with terrorism and its terrible consequences for society and polity in every part of the world. There is 9/11 associated with our own history which conveyed a sublime message and heralded a new age of reconstruction and reconciliation anchored on non-violent action. We are less aware of that 9/11. It was on this day in 1893 that Swami Vivekananda delivered his historic lecture at the World Parliament of Religions in Chicago cautioning the world about the danger posed by fanaticism and hoping that the bloodshed and violence caused by the fanatic elements would not occur in future. Thirteen years later, that is, on 9/ 11, 1906, Mahatma Gandhi started his first Satyagraha which was unprecedented in history in harnessing the soul force and spiritualism for the fighting for freedom and democratic rights of Indians who were deprived of these basic rights because of the colour of their skin. It is well-known that the first Satyagraha was the first step for our non-violent struggle for independence and a more remarkable step in the history of mankind for restructuring the world on the basis of the non-violent method. It continued for eight years and its ever lasting significance and relevance beyond time and space make it a rarest of the rare revolutionary event in history.

The might, majesty and beauty of the first Satyagraha can be found in its broad scope which encompassed diverse themes and which are of immense relevance for our own time. The first and foremost message of the first Satyagraha is harmony, tolerance and solidarity of different religions. The Hindus, Muslims, Parsis and Christians participated in it and fought for their common rights by learning and applying the methods of self-restraint, sacrifice and respect for one another's faith. The denomination of a person, instead of coming on the way of a concerted movement, became a cementing factor and contributed to its onward progress. During the freedom movement Mahatma Gandhi repeatedly referring to the first Satyagaraha used to say that adherence to truth and non-violence enabled the Satyagrahis to see beauty in each and every religion. In fact it is instructive to note that Muslims remained in the forefront of the first Satyagraha and they never gave priority to their religious identity over their other identities and stressed on the larger cause at the heart of which remained the Indian identity.

Today when fanatic elements are causing divisions in our society on the basis of religion and asking our Muslim brothers and sisters to prove their patriotism let us recall the message of the first Satyagraha arid refashion our own approach to understand their commitment to the cause of India.

It is of utmost importance to know that when Mahatma Gandhi, the architect of the first Satyagraha, fell unconscious uttering *Hey Ram* after he was fatally attacked by Muslims for compromising on the issue of registration of Indians under the prevailing law by giving finger prints, he issued an appeal to the Hindus in South Africa not to get agitated. He asked for restraint and requested them not to put themselves on the wrong side. Gandhiji did not plead for the prosecution of those who attacked him. It is this spirit of broadminded approach eschewing retaliatory attitude that is of critical relevance for the twenty-first century world marked by violence due to advocacy of the action reaction theory by the communal and fascist forces. This is the age of geo-economics. Competition in trade and commerce is the defining aspect of this age. It is fascinating to recall that Indians faced discrimination in South Africa primarily because the White settlers there could not compete with the Indians in reaping better profits in the world of business. It sounds strange that Indians hundred years back with the disadvantage of education, technical skill, colour of the skin and above all of absence of political power were beating the British people in the field of business. Gandhiji in his book, *Satyagraha in South Africa,* has written that had Indians remained in the condition of semi-slavery without challenging the monopoly of British settlers on trade, the rights of Indians would not have been adversely affected by legislative measures. He wrote:

> To nip the political power of Indians in the bud was for them the indispensable first step; but the real point of attack was Indian trade and free Indian immigration.

Hundred years after the first Satyagraha India is emerging as a major economic player in the world and the whole world is watching India with trepidation because of the competitive ability of Indians in showing remarkable business acumen and registering impressive success in the field of trade and commerce. President George Bush in his. State of the Union Address referred to the competition from India and appealed to the people of the USA to boldly face it. Let us reverentially pay our tribute to Mahatma Gandhi and all those who participated in the first Satyagraha in 1906 for the inalienable rights of the Indians for doing business.

One of the striking aspects of the 9/11,1906 was the way Indians and Chinese came together to fight against discrimination. Mahatma Gandhi has acknowledged that without the participation of the Chinese residents of Johannesburg the Satyagraha would not have been successful. In fact, the Chinese along with Indians were asked to obtain licence to do business in South Africa. It was the common cause of business which brought them together in South Africa hundred years back. In the twenty-first century both the countries are in the forefront of a world the contours of which are determined by the increasing value and volume of trade and commerce. I recall Deng Xiaopeng who said that without India and China coming together, the twenty-first century cannot be made the century of the Asia-Pacific. The seeds of making the twenty-first century an Asia Pacific century were sown when India and China were united together in 1906 and fought for their genuine rights. That spirit has to be recaptured to revitalise our relations and restore the spiritual basis of our material progress.

We are familiar with the theory of clash of civilisations advocated by the eminent scholar, Prof. Samuel Huntington. It is a dangerous theory which sees different civilisations in antagonistic terms. The same was advocated by General Smuts in South Africa when Mahatma Gandhi was spearheading the first Satyagraha. When Indians fought against the restrictions imposed on them for their entry into Transvaal, General Smuts said:

> South Africa is a representative Western civilisation while India is the centre of Oriental culture. Thinkers of the present generation hold that these two civilisations cannot go together. If nations representing these rival cultures meet even in small groups, the result will only be an explosion.

Mahatma Gandhi described such argument as pseudo-philosophical and said that oriental civilisation not only does not fear but positively welcomes free contact with Westen civilisation. What Huntington said was an extension of what General Smuts articulated in 1906. When the exclusivist approach to culture and civilisation is being revived, the world view of Mahatma Gandhi that civilisations could come in contact and coexist is of practical necessity for our world troubled by the upsurge of fanaticism and terrorism. It is this transcendental message of the first Satyagraha that has to be part of our consciousness and guide our actions.

With the commencement of the first Satyagraha began the age of common man. In South Africa it was Mahatma Gandhi who started consulting the ordinary indentured labours and illiterate people for preparing petitions to the government to redress their grievances. Everybody was stunned by Gandhiji's approach. He replied that brain splitting was not the monopoly of the educated people alone. He consciously mingled with the illiterate and neglected labourers and enlisted their support for the cause of the Satyagraha. In his autobiography, My *Experiments with Truth,* and in his book, *Satyagraha in South Africa,* he has given copious references to the role played by ordinary people in subjecting themselves to suffering for the cause of the rights of the Indians. It was by freely mixing with the coolies and labourers that Mohandas Karamchand Gandhi learnt to further simplify his own life and lead the life of the humblest of the human beings. Recognising the potentiality of the ordinary people he wrote:

> In my opinion there is no place on earth and no race which is not capable of producing the finest types of humanity, given suitable opportunities and education.

The ideal and practice of serving the common people and nurturing their talents need to be invoked to make our democracy more meaningful for the vast masses of people living across the length and breadth of our country.

One of the enduring lessons of the first Satyagraha is to respect modem Indian languages. During the thick of the Satyagraha Mahatma Gandhi adorned the role of a teacher. Since large number of the participants were from Tamil Nadu he started learning the Tamil language. In the Phoenix settlement he taught the children of the indentured labourers by using their mother tongues. He later wrote that while fighting for the rights of the Indians I also fought for the cause of the languages of India. In fact Mahatma Gandhi did not send any of his children to public schools where education was being imparted in English. He wrote that the mind which is not crushed by the burden of learning a foreign tongue during the childhood days is the freest of the brains which can later pick up any language and acquire any type of education. In the age of extinction of many languages when linguists are pleading for preserving the diverse heritage of language and literature the message of the first Satyagarha is of far-reaching significance.

The twenty-first century is witnessing the return of infectious diseases. The main reason for the emergence of this kind of problem is the modem life-style and pursuit of greed. The first Satyagraha teaches us the lesson of simplicity and the rules of health and hygiene. With his uncanny understanding of the living condition of Indians Mahatma Gandhi asked them to remain clean, eschew unhygienic practices and separate their business establishments from their residential premises. Now the Supreme Court of India is stressing on the fact that shops must not be established in the residential areas. Mahatma Gandhi did so hundred years back. How far ahead Mahatma Gandhi was! By educating people to follow these practices he was, in his own words, "preparing people for participating in Satyagraha." Much later he exhorted Indians to maintain the highest standards of cleanliness and put the subject of rural sanitation in his constructive programme. His priority on cleanliness was amply reflected in his statement: "If we do not keep our backwards clean our *swaraj* will have a foul stench." Let us examine, if we have been successful in removing the stench that has plagued us for long.

Accountability is the defining feature of making our public life more democratic and clean. It is amazing to know that the first Satyagraha was a Satyagraha for accountability. Gandhiji, while collecting funds and spending them, kept detailed accounts and subjected them to scrutiny. What he has written in his book, *Satyagraha in South Africa,* concerning accountability, is not only revealing but also instructive. He wrote:

> For the benefit of young aspirants after public work, I note down the fact that we were so punctilious in keeping the accounts... that we preserved even SUC! trifling vouchers as the receipts for the money spent in the steamers upon say soda water. Similarly we preserved the receipts for telegrams. I do not remember to have entered a single item under sundries when writing the detailed accounts we must account for every single pie... If such is the responsibility in private life, in public life it is all the greater. Keeping accounts is an independent duty, the performance of which is essential to clean work, and if the leading workers of the institution which we voluntarily serve do not ask us for accounts out of a sense of false courtesy or fear, they too are equally to blame. If a paid servant is bound to account for work done and money spent by him. The volunteer is doubly bound to do so, for his work is as a reward to him. This is a very important matter, and as I know that this is generally not sufficiently attended to in many institutions

The erosion of accountability is a major reason for the decline of governance. Mahatma Gandhi had set a shining example of accountability hundred years back. Let us follow that example and restore cleanliness in public life.

ANOTHER remarkable aspect of the first Satyagraha is the way Gandhi used the media for educating public opinion. The newspaper *Indian Opinion* was the product of the first Satyagraha. It was established by Mahatma Gandhi and was being run without advertisements. The whole community was participating in the management of the *Indian Opinion*. It was a refreshing example of a newspaper which did not get bogged down by the pressures of the market and profit motives. Mahatma Gandhi used it to teach people the rules of health and hygiene and make them aware of their political rights. The broad-spectrum objective of the newspaper distinguished it as a paper for freedom and social reform. Its legacy has to be recaptured to restore the credibility of the media which is suffering erosion due to the departure from the path of truth and objectivity.

Without reflecting on the role played by women in the first Satyagraha its assessment will not be complete. Large numbers of women participated in the first Satyagraha when a court of law in South Africa delivered a judgement that the marriages solemnised without Christian tradition were illegal. It infuriated women. They courted arrest under the leadership of Mahatma Gandhi and some of them died due to the harsh treatment they received in jail. They marched long distances with their babies in their arms and had to subject themselves to unbearable difficulties. A lady while crossing a river lost her child when he fell into the river from her arms. But she kept marching on for the larger cause of Satyagraha. Another sixteen-year-old girl Valliamma went to jail, was infected with severe cold, became a skeleton due to illness in jail and eventually died. Mahatma Gandhi was stunned by her courage when she said: "I want to go to jail and die for the motherland." When she breathed her last Gandhiji wrote:

> She left us the heritage of an immortal name... And the name of Valliamma will live in the history of South Africa Satyagraha as long as India lives... None can tell whose sacrifice in South Africa was acceptable to God, and hence bore fruit. But we do know that Valliamma's sacrifice bore fruit and so did the sacrifice of the other sisters.

It is a remarkable tribute to the woman of India who remained in the forefront of the first ever non-violent struggle for freedom, dignity and independence. Today when women are themselves struggling for their rights the spirit of the first Satyagraha will influence them to march ahead to realise their objectives in practice and in full measure.

One of the most creative interpretations of the Satyagraha in South Africa traces the intellectual lineage of the post-modern society in the *Hind Swarajj* written by Mahatma Gandhi during the Satyagraha. It was a critique of the modern civilisation. By launching the Satyagraha in South Africa and subsequently fighting for the independence of India. Mahatma Gandhi was criticising the civilisation which multiplied wants while laying the foundation of a post-modern society. This he did by stressing on bread labour, manual work, restoring the Panchayats, using appropriate technology and, above all, addressing the concerns of the poorest of the poor and the marginalised sections of society. The book, *Post-Modern Gandhi and Other Essays,* written by Rudolph and Rudolph, gives an account of the way Mahatma Gandhi became the founder of the post-modem society. Indeed the unmistakable processes of the post-modem society could be traced in the dynamics of the first Satyagraha. Mahatma Gandhi's vision indeed went beyond colonial modernity and embraced the more universal vision of humanism and spiritualism. The first Satyagraha, started on 9/11, 1906, conveys us the meaning which goes beyond democratic and political rights and embrace the larger goal of freeing the world from the monstrous greed of materialism. No wonder therefore that Leo Tolstoy, referring to Mahatma Gandhi's Satyagraha in South Africa, wrote in 1910:

> Your work in the Transvaal which seems to be far away from the centre of our world, is yet the most fundamental and most important to us, supplying the most weighty practical proof in which the world now can share and with which we must participate, not only the Christians but all the peoples of the world.

Let US all strive for building a more inclusive India and the world by following the ideals of the first Satyagraha.

21

Economics of Ahimsa, Technology and Environment: Relevance of Gandhiji

Dr. B. Madhukar and Mr. G. Surya Prakasa Rao

Introduction

An economic organization refer to how we produce Material goods, how we distribute them from producers to consumers and how we consume them in order to sustain and reproduce ourselves. We are also going to critique our modern industrial way of organizing production, distribution and consumption, as well as the economic theories that have arisen to defend this system. First that industrial capitalism in a violent system whose roots lie in the history of colonial disregard for nature and for other humans. Second that despite political decolonization, we have not yet economically declonized ourselves and modern economics shows evidence of this in the way it conceptualizes the relationship between humans and nature. And third that the Economics of Ahimsa, as developed by Gandhi, Kumarappa and other in response to the violence of industrial càpitalization. The idea that our ethical or moral values should govern our economic decisions is itself not new at all. But Gandhiji once said that non-violence was as old as the hills. But hopefully we will be able to present it somewhat of a new light here.

Gandhiji, Kumarappa and the Economics of Ahimsa

In modern times and particularly in the west, Ahimsa in most closely associated with the name of Mahatma Gandhi. Gandhi's anti-imperialist struggle against the British Raj in India and his philosophy of Ahimsa are better known than his economic ideas. And yet he was very concerned with what would today be called development and modernization. Gandhi's economic ideas flowed naturally from his ethics and politics. Restriction of wants, self-reliance and economic equality, which we will discuss today in the economic context. But in post-colonial period of India, Gandhi's economic ideas are only a nominal part of official economic policy. However, an investigation into Gandhian economic thought has made itself felt as a part of the growing literature on heterodox economics.

J.C. Kumarappa was a contemporary of Gandhi who independently developed ideas similar to Gandhiji's. After return to India with an M.A in Economics from Columbia University, Kumarappa became Gandhi's co-worker and led the All India Village Industries Association for many years. Being a trained economist, Kumarappa was the official economic voice of the Gandhian village movement. Live Gandhiji, he recognized that India's village industries, based on low- cost, labour- intensive, low-environmental impact technologies, and decentralized production, were crucial to restoring wealth and dignity to the masses. Two of his books outline his major ideas:

"Economy of Permanence: a quest for a social order based on non-violence" and "why the village movement?" Besides these, two he wrote many other books and articles of both theoretical and practical nature. In his books Kumarappa criticizes economics that places excessive importance on material growth and ever-increasing standards of living. The type of economy that finds most favour with Kumarappa is one in which nature's cycles are disturbed to a minimal extent by human activity. This is directly opposed to views articulated by luminaries of the European Enlightenment. Such as Francis Bacon, who talked more of subjugating nature to human needs than living in harmony with her. Of course, Gandhi and Kumarappa are by no means the only people who articulated a view of human-nature relationship that stress balance and co-operation over control and conflict. The idea is prominent for example in Native American critiques of industrialism, to name but one. We can trace Kumarappa's influence in the thought of British economist, Fritz Schumacher. In his famous book, " Small is Beautiful: A study of Economics as if People Mattered", Schumacher says:

> "From the economic point of view, the central concept of wisdom is permanence. We must study the economics of permanence. Nothing makes sense unless it's continuance for a long time can be projected without running into absurdities. There can be growth towards a limited objective but there cannot be unlimited, generalized growth."

We have already heard much about the concept of Ahimsa. So we will restrict my self to only a few relevant comments here. Ahimsa has been translated into English as "non-violence", but it entails much more than the mere negation of violence. It is sometimes translated more appropriately as "love". It is a positive idea that stands for a way of life that emphasizes simple living without going undue violence to the earth and its creatures. Gandhi once said: "That economics is untrue which ignores or disregards moral values." Similarly, Kumarappa, in "Economy of Permanence", remarks, "an economy that is based purely on monetary or material standards of value, does not take a realistic perspective in Time and Space. This short coming leads to a blind alley of violence and destruction from which there is no escape."

There are several components to Gandhi's and Kumarappa's theory. For, developing my own critique here I will focus mostly on their critique of "machine civilization" as inherently violent, and their concepts of swadeshi or the principle of local economy and aparigraha, the principle of minimization of wants or simplification of material life. The economics of Ahimsa stresses local, decentralized community economies and economies of needs rather than wants. By de-emphasizing production for sake of production, consumption for sake of consumption or growth for sake of growth, it also tackles the thorny issue of how to achieve a basic material level of comfort for all without compromising the viability of future generations, or what has come to be called "sustainable development ", Several aspects of this critique and the alternatives offered are to be found in various traditions all over the world, and especially those coming from the colonized peoples in the Americas, in Asia and Africa.

Capitalism and The Enlightenment Roots of Modern Economics

The Economics of Ahimsa is a response, not just to the science of Modern Economics, but to the very way in which human society organizes itself and interacts with nature today. Moreover, it is a response to the legacy of 300 or more years of capitalism. The Ahimsa perspective recognizes that, as a system of organizing our material life, industrial capitalism has failed spectacularly. We live with exploitation and alienation in the work place; we see extreme poverty alongside extreme wealth, centralization of economic and political power, fragmentation of the family and division of humanity along endless fractures of class, race and ethnicity. Further, we have depleted and polluted our natural resources to unprecedented levels and global climate change is a reality to all but the most die -hard skeptics. We have turned our ecological and intellectual commons into commodities to be sold for profit to the point where none of us feels there is anything strange about buying water in plastic bottles or patenting words and phrases in the English language or denying farmers the right to replant their own seeds.

How did we end-up here? The story has been told many times. The First Industrial Revolution in England in the later of the 18th century marked the culmination of the ideas developed during the European Enlightenment. With the invention of steam and coal powered machinery man was said to have " mastered nature" or become its sovereign. This particular form of knowledge being generated during the Enlightenment was convenient for an economic system that needed nature to be just another commoditable asset. Of course, land like labour did not become a commodity without their land and work. But in the end force and violence triumphed. One cannot talk of the industrial colonialism, slavery, massive looting of natural resources and decimation of entire populations via disease, starvation and war. It was a short step to bind into service and make slave, not just nature, but also other humans who failed for reasons of primitiveness, race or toilet habits to make it into the group that did the controlling and the binding. As Sahasrabudhey has pointed out, it has been a truism in economics at least since Adam Smith that modern industry creates wealth. However, those living in Asia, Africa and the Americas saw wealth being destroyed or stolen not created. Having briefly talked about the origins of industrial capitalism and its relationship to modern economics, let us move to the specific domains of production, distribution and consumption.

Production

The dramatic increase in productive power associated with rise of capitalism has given rise to a fetish of productivity, an emphasis on endless production. The promise of production saturates the air everywhere. Thus for economists of almost all hues, technology has become an object of worship, yielding ever more commodities at lower and lower visible costs and enabling more consumption, hence a higher standard of living. The Ahimsa perspective discussed here is the perspective of those civilizations that have born the invisible costs of industrialization. It thus questions whether industrial civilization which in its present form is so reliant on technology that does violence to man and nature, is at all capable of being non-violent, or in balance with nature.

Technology

Gandhi, commenting on Jawaharlal Nehru's socialist beliefs, once said, "Pandit Nehru wants industrialization because he thinks that if it is socialized, it would be free from the evils of capitalism. The evils are inherent in industrialism and no amount of socialization can eradicate them." This is a fundamental difference between a Marxist critique of capitalism and a Gandhian critique based on Ahimsa. The Marxist view of machines simply tools that can be put to good or bad use depending upon the social relations of production often seems reasonable to people like us who are so used to technology in our lives. By contrast Gandhi's views on technology have been attacked as being primitive and unrealistic. Even in Gandhi's own time his opposition to the violence of large-scale industry was unpopular to say the least. Although he did temper the radical views of his youth later in life, one may argue that his position is not based on a moral fundamentalism, as has been suggested, but on understanding of the hidden costs, environmental and human, of modern technology.

Gandhi supported what has later been called appropriated technology or intermediate technology. Low cost, labour intensive rather than capital intensive, production that did not disturb nature's balance in a large way, did not have a large ecological footprint. In the realm of production, he valorized the Indian handicraft industry and made the spinning – wheel or charkha the symbol of his activity. To the urban intelligentsia with a modern education, it was hard to believe that the subjugated and ruined Indian society had much of value to offer in terms of inspiration for how to organize industry in the modern age. Subsequent work by historians like Dharampal, have borne out Gandhi's views on many aspects of the socio-economic organization of Indian society. Although the Nehruvian vision of large dams and massive state-owned industry triumphed in the official realm of policy, the Gandhian vision has survived to this day. It has provided the inspiration for micro hydel projects that bring electricity to a few villages by constructing small check dams, for watershed management projects that attempt to replenish the ground water in arid areas using low-cost technology etc., and for many environmental struggles against the degradation caused by modern technology. This Ahimsa vision has also promoted some to look to the surviving Indian artisanal tradition for inspiration on how to organize production in a non-violent fassion. One example is the long neglected process of steel manufacture with small clay furnaces that was widely prevalent in north India but has since fallen into disuse. Of course, it is not being suggested that we can use this process to supply the world's steel needs today. It is merely a lesson in how production has historically been organized in less violent ways and the resources that will still be available to humanity when the sweep of modernity is over.

A second somewhat under emphasized aspect of Gandhiji's critique of the machine is regarding the nature of work in modern societies. Much has been said about the alienating nature of work under capitalism and the violence done to the human pysche as a result of deskilled, menial labour. Not surprisingly then, neo-classical economics regards work as a disutility, i.e. something that causes unhappiness and that it to be avoided as much as possible. A rational individual is supposed to maximize leisure time and minimize work. The Ahimsa perspective, in contrast, pays great attention to how man reacts to his own work and does not regard work as a chore. Kumarappa notes, "Our daily round of duties is as much a part of ourselves as our physical body. Man expressed himself by his work and at the same time builds his personality by his acts ..." hence, the occupation we follow is not merely a means of earnings our daily bread.

Distribution

Distribution refers to the movement of inputs to producers and outputs to consumers. In an economy where production occurs purely for use, the problem of how to distribute does not arise because the producers of a good or a service are themselves the users. A completely materially self-sufficient individual or even family is rarity and most societies have some form of exchange. The movement exchange enters the picture the producer is distanced from the consumer. The principle of local economy or swadeshi insists on minimizing this distance. Local economies have been discussed extensively as alternatives to globalization. For Gandhi, swadeshi is response to the capitalist global economy that results in colonialism and imperialism. As Lenin made famous in his pamphlet on imperialism, the endless search for cheap raw materials, cheap labour and newer markets for manufacturing goods is a prime cause for wars under capitalism. The link between wars and environmental degradation can easily be imagined. Swadeshi emphasized production for local use and consumption of locally manufactured goods in order to avoid the violence that accompanies international trade. The Swadeshi theory of trade is radically different from trade theories in neo-classical economics. The most famous one being the theory of comparative advantage that emphasized mutual gains from trade purely in terms of greater consumption. Thus, the neo-classical motto is "Some trade is better than no trade." While the Swadeshi motto is "no trade is better than exploitative trade."

The doctrine of swadeshi recognizes that the value of a good or service cannot be reduced to its price but that human and environmental conditions involved in its manufacture matter as much if not more. Anticipating the days of consumer awareness and local currency, Kumarappa had the following list of questions ready for all consumers. "What does one know about where the article comes from? Who makes the article? From what material? Under what conditions do the workers live and work? What be seen, these questions are easier to answer for participants of an economy that produces mainly for the local market. Kumarappa explains the moral basis of swadeshi as follows. "Those of us who apply human standards of value (to production) have to inquire into all aspects of manufacture. It is an arduous task and it becomes almost impossible for ordinary persons to undertake it when the articles come from far off countries."

There are two common objections to swadeshi. First, it has sometimes been (mis) interpreted as an insistence on complete economic self-sufficiency for a nation or a community. Swadeshi, as a conceived by Gandhi does not reject trade with other nations or communities in Toto but it is opposed to an international order based solely on considerations of comparative advantage or a system that celebrates global trade for its own sake or for the sake of profit maximization (what is euphemistically called *competitiveness*). Second, like in Marxist economics, the principle of non-exploitation in part of the Economics of Ahimsa and it entails that the product of a worker's labour is not appropriated by a capitalist or a landlord who has done nothing to produce it, but retained by the worker herself. Thus swadeshi is not simply capitalism with local capitalists instead of global ones but also calls for a change in the way in which production is socially organized.

Even if the will is present, serious questions still remain as to how a swadeshi economy can survive in today's globalized world. With the information and communications Revolution of the 1990s and the relentless expansion of the neo-liberal model of economic organization, arguing for a swadeshi economy in 2006 seems anachronistic, even ridiculous. Nevertheless, interesting experiments are being carried out in local economy management and they serve as models for more such efforts. Some of you may be aware of the work being done on various aspects of local economy by folks at the Schumacher society. I will also briefly mention one such experiment being carried out in southern India, under the relationship of Rangaswamy Elango, in the town of Kuthambakkam. Elango is working on establishing a land / agriculture based local economy, along the lines of the products that are consumed by the villagers can be produced locally. Elango estimated, through detailed door-to-door survey by his team, that 5/6 of the commodities that kuthambakkam consumes every month could be produced within the village and traded locally. While experiments such as Elango's are by far the exception rather than the norm, they can still be an inspiration for anyone wishing to create alternatives.

Consumption

Utility Maximization and Capital Accumulation or Aparigraha

In the context of economic growth, modern economics regards more material goods to be better. With this emphasis on growth in production naturally comes an emphasis on increasing consumption. Consumption is theorized in neo-classical economics under the name of the utility maximization theory of consumer demand. We can think of utility as happiness. But greater utility is derived, in this theory, from the consumption of more commodities. The definition of a rational person, in consumer theory, is someone who derives greater happiness from consuming more subject to his or her budget constraint. Moreover, in this theory, the preferences of an individual are taken as given and unchanging. There is no recognition that an individual may modify his or her wants in accordance with extra -economic principles such as ethical or moral values. In contrast to utility maximization and ever increasing wants. The Economics of Ahimsa emphasizes aparigraha, or non-possession has the ideal to strive. Aparigraha, is an ancient concept in Jain spiritual thought, as indeed is Ahimsa Gandhi summarizes the motivation for aparigraha thus in " Hind Swaraj." "We notice that the mind is a restless bird: the more it gets the more it wants, and still remains unsatisfied. The more we indulge our passions the more unbridled they become. " Simplicity and non-violence are closely related to caring for the environment. Producing a high degree of human satisfaction by means of a relatively how rate of consumption allows people to live without great pressure on the environment or on their fellow humans.

It is important here to deal with two common objections. First, these thoughts may strike us as being too idealistic. It should be pointed out that we do not posit minimization of wants or renunciation of material comforts to be the only motivating force behind an individual's actions. But neither are we willing to cede all economic acts to the domain of self-interest or rational greed. Here, as in swadeshi, what matters is a genuine desire to strive towards the respective ideals, knowing that one may never completely achieve them. Second, neither Gandhiji nor Kumarappa glorified poverty, as they are commonly accused of doing. Rather than telling the poor to be happy in their poverty, they are telling the rich that more wealth will not bring greater happiness. Gandhi called poverty a sin and his system of political economy was intended to eradicate India's poverty and bring about parity of wealth. Ajit Dasgupta, in his book on Gandhian Economics, has pointed out that "Doctrines calling for limitation of wants can easily be construed as an attempt at ideological justification of the status quo. However, even a preliminary reading of Gandhi should make it clear that he was anything but status quoits. His doctrine is rather 'Sarvodaya' or what we might call in modern parlance. "An exercise in the optimization of overall individual welfare. Thus, speaking on the theme of material and moral progress, Gandhi emphasizes that:

> "No one has ever suggested that grinding pauperism can lead to anything else than moral degradation. Every human being has a right to live and therefore to find the where withal to feed himself and where necessary to clothe and house himself. But, for this very simple performance, we need to assistance from economists or their laws... The only statement that has to be examined is whether is can be laid down as a law of universal application that materiel advancement means moral progress."

Needless to say Gandhi rejects the law that material advancement means moral progress.

Conclusions

Let us close with a few general observations. Whenever we criticize technology we open ourselves to allegations of primitivism, increasing poverty etc. This is an obstacle to seriously questioning the violence of industrial modernity within the framework of modern economics. But the all -too-frequently-heard modernist criticism of Gandhian ideas, that they threaten to turn the clock back or take us into a "pre-modern past" only makes sense within the modernist conception of progress but not if we reject it.

In the foregoing pages we have tried to simultaneously critique the biases in modern economics in the domains of production, distribution and consumption, while attempting to present an alternative vision from the perspective of Ahimsa. Ahimsa can guide not only our individual actions in everyday life but also our struggle for making possible other worlds. This perspective also gives us new eyes to see the future in the present. Entire worlds of human activity not based on violence but instead on non-violent co-operation, on the logic of the gift and on caring become visible to us. The truth is that even with all its violence capitalism and industrialism never did conquer all domains of human activity, or even all aspects of economic activity. In answer to the rhetoric that "There is No

Alternative Rhetoric" emanating from the centres of powers we can say that not only are Other Worlds possible, they already exist here and now.

REFERENCES

1. Schumacher, E.F. (1973), *Small is Beautiful: A Study of Economics as a People Mattered* (Harper and Row, New York 1973).
2. Kumarappa, J.C. (1945), Economy of Performance.
3. Basole, A. (2005), *The Economics of Ahimsa: Gandhi,* Kumarappa and the Non-Modern Challenges to Economics.
4. Dasgupta, A.K., (1996), Gandhi's Economic Thought.
5. Lenin, V.I. (1915/1939), *Imperialism: The Highest Stage of Capitalism.*
6. Kumarappa, J.C. (1968), Swadeshi: The moral law of Self-Reliance.
7. Gandhi, M.K. (1908), *Hind Swaraj or Indian Home Rule* (Navajivan Publishing House, Ahmadabad, 2001).

22

Gandhian Views on Khadi Clothing

K. Visweswara Rao and A.V. Jogarao

Roman gold, says history, paid for the import of Indian textiles, while Alexander the Great, when he invaded the country in 327 BC, was dazzled by the art of fabric making and printing as also was marco polo the Venetian traveller. It was in 1921 that Gandhi launched the movement of spin your own cloth and buy hand spun cloth which gained momentum making khadi the fabric of the freedom struggle.

Around that time Gandhi used khadi as the uniform for the first Non-cooperation movement and the Gandhi cap had strong symbolic overtones – that of the Indo-British battle over the looms of Manchester and a bid for a modern Indian identity. So deep rooted was the sentiment attached to this fabric that Pandit Nehru wove for his daughter Indira a wedding sari in salmon pink khadi while he was in jail. This sari is still worn by women of the Nehru-Gandhi family on their wedding day.

The first true Indian designer was Mahatma Gandhi when he urged the people of India to wear khadi garments. It was not only a call to create self-reliance but a call to wear something that could prove the unity of India. Khadi was given a more important status by Gandhi after his return from South Africa. While in search of the Charkha, Gandhi felt that for a nation to turn self-reliant, it had to return to indigenous manufactured goods.

Gandhi wrote, Swaraj (self-rule) without swadeshi (country made goods) is a lifeless corpse and if swadeshi is the soul of swaraj, khadi is the essence of swedeshi. Therefore, khadi became not only a symbol of revolution and resistance but part of an Indian identity.

The weaving of khadi is preceded by the spinning of the thread on the charkha after which it goes to the bobbin winder, warper, sizer and finally the weaver. While spinning is organized by the Khadi Board, weaving is done by the weaver at his home in an individual capacity. Spinning is mostly done by the girls and women in the villages, while weaving is dominated by men. Because of the work involved, the price of the khadi cloth when it reaches the shops is more than that of the mill or handloom cloth.

Khadi over the decades has moved from a freedom fighter's identity fabric to a fashion garment. At one time it was scorned as fabric for the farmer and the rural wearer. Today there is such an increasing demand for khadi cloth that despite the million workers all over the country involved in spinning it they are unable to meet the demands of the market.

In 1990 designer Ritu Kumar of Delhi presented her first khadi collection at the Crafts Museum. Her tree of life show, an audio-visual tableau spanning the history of textiles in India, showed the design lexicon of the country, the creators of textiles, those who have regenerated textile crafts and those who would wear the garments.

Eight collection were presented of which khadi was a very significant one. Since then the tree of life show has been presented several times for charity and caused a stir with its creations. Once again in 1997, Ritu Kumar presented the tree of life shown this time in London where the British were amazed with her khadi collections.

Once the sign of freedom, Khadi today holds it own on the fashion scene......it is a part of every wardrobe when it comes to selecting fabric with a discerning eye, informs Ritu Kumar.

Today the younger generation may draw inspiration from the way film and MTV stars are dressing, but there was a time when fashion too was dictated by our political leaders more than the dresses it was what they signified and the fiery personalities behind them that caught the imagination of the masses and influenced them to unwaveringly follow the footsteps of their leaders, even in adapting the way they dressed, recalls Ritu Kumar.

Khadi, over the 50 years, has taken interesting—and I should say irrational-twists and turns.

First myth about Khadi:it helps the poor. According to Gandhi, the poor don't really need your help. But for argument sake, let's say that the city folks want to wear khadi; they don't have the time or the inclination to spin it, but they want to buy it. So, government steps in and says, "Ah, we can do employment generation with Khadhi."Annually, 600 crores (6 billion) rupees of Khadi is purchased by consumers, so perhaps that money can employ the 40 per cent unemployed villagers of India.

But since khadi is woven by hand in villages it is often difficult to provide large quantities of the fabric at short notice. Yet it is this handmade quality of the fabric with its inherent defects that is the beauty of khadi and that is what the buyer wants at times. Says kamal it is not a poor man's fabric although it provides employment to the poor man. It is a very up-market fabric emphasizes khadi dhotis are turned into printed kurtas and dupattas.

There are times when the price and coarseness of the fabric deterred the fashion conscious from wearing it. But today khadi has many faces which are not just restricted to cotton. There is khadi is quite competitive now and depending on the style of the garment it could range between Rs. 400-2500.

Technology, innovation, efficiency is not to be discarded. But if these advances are created in profit-making silos, it annihilates the cultural fabric of an ecosystem and eventually, runs the risk of destroying the entire eco-system itself.

When most people think of cotton, they think white . No one in this generation will even remember that cotton naturally grows in many other colours like brown and yellow. Because of the heavy textile demand for white cotton, all farmers started producing white cotton. Moreover, the heavy cotton consumption by the mills created an imbalance in the natural ecology as a result, 80 per cent of all pesticides used in Indian farms are used on cotton farms Eighty per cent.

To "efficiently" transport cotton to centralized mills, it is compressed. Then, at the farms, lots of energy is spent in carding the cotton to make it fluffy again.

Most khadi producers now use "new and improved" Amber-charka in India. You can't blame the producers in a land where more than 350 million people live on less than dollar a day; they are just trying to survive. But the confusion of the government policies, technologists and pundits are creating these weird hybrid solutions that are simply not khadi. Not only are Ambar-charka machine parts hard to maintain, it also requires long-staple cotton silver that is used by textile mills. The same long-staple cotton that has increased the use of pesticides, destroyed cotton bio-diversity, and created many subtle forms of inefficiencies. So this kind of a khadi movement is far cry from Gandhi's vision of self-reliance.

Gandhi once said," Live simply, so others can simply live." His interest wasn't in selling khadi and marketing consumerism. He wanted the common man to be self-reliant, to be free from market forces to think for himself, to be alive in ways that are natural to them. Perhaps Gandhi's message is too revolutionary for our times.

At present, Khadi is a bit more expensive today and that can change with the right policies and better marketing still, just as an original painting will never be as cheap as a print, hand-spun khadi and block printing won't ever be able to compete with a 80 rupee t-shirt made from synthetic material. But if production of the chemical dyes used to colour our t-shirts will ruin the rivers, if the mass cotton production will ruin the land, and the lack of jobs will ruin the lives of the common man, the questions really is it worth it? No one in their right minds will think so.

Root of the problem, though, is that "khadi" itself is in a state of mess. Gandhians have become idealists whose message is largely disregarded by the consumeristic mainstream. Village producers are just trying to make their daily livelihood. Consumers are getting mixed signals from the government policies, propaganda and competition attempts against the textile industry; to top it off, no one has paid any attention to fashion in khadi. Government is trying to increase jobs and provide rebates but the khadi commission itself admitted, "our biggest problems is that we don't know how to get the help to the right person," that is to say, there is no infrastructure to implement policies.

Process of Making Khadi

1. Farming : pick your own cotton.
2. Ginning: remove the seeds and roll up a silver of cotton.

3. Spinning : use the silver and a manual "charkha", to create yarn.
4. Weaving: weave the yarn into cloth.
5. Stiching:tailor clothes from the yarn.

Encourage Khadi Fabric and Discourage Synthethic Fabric

Gandhiji encouraged people to wear khadi by being an example himself. Even today it is relevant in the Indian context. When people take to wearing khadi, rural employment will be generated as the khadi industry is mainly rural based. Not only this, it will benefit the formers as they can sell the cotton produced direct to the cottage industry which is there in the villages itself. Middle men will be avoided and the farmers will be a happier lot. The distress factor of the farmers as well as wevers can also be reduced and suicide cases will definitely come down.

In an individual wears 3 mts of khadi cloth in a year, is indirectly benefits a cultivator, a weaver, a tailor and a trader. Not only these four people get employment for one-day, their dependents taken on an average to be members (2 to 4) get food or a square meal for a day.

REFERENCES

1. Khadi Village and Industries Commission (KVIC).
2. An Autobiography of Ghandiji.
3. The Collected Works of Gandhiji (January-February).

23

Total Prohibition of Alcohol Consumption: Gandhian Ideology

Dr. B. Madhukar and Mr. G. Surya Prakasa Rao

Introduction

The Problem of Alcoholism is not a new one. Alcohol consumption was considered as a vice way back even in the history. It seems to be an intractable problem everytime, in the present and in the olden days too. It is only the degree of the problem and its impact on the society, which is talked more in the policies. While state's concentration is on the revenue it generates, the physician's concentration is on the cost of servicing the problems caused by Alcohol. Thus in a developing country like India, the problem has been transformed into a problem of National economy, government policy and social reforms.

Today, after experiencing one and half decades of globalism, the status of alcoholism in the India needs no separate mention. In recent years, alcohol consumption has greatly increased. Especially among urban literate households. Some statistics say that, by 2001, the number of drinkers has increased from one in 300 (1980's) to one in 20. Further, this vice in found to be increasing especially among young professionals who regard drinking as a fashion and as part of being modern.

It is in this context, a small attempt is made here, to recall the Gandhian ideas, which highlighted the need for a dry India free from the clutches of Alcoholism.

The Career of Prohibition as a Government Policy in India

The early British Policy relating to liquor consumption was of three dimensions:

1. To minimize temptation to those who do not drink,
2. To discourage excess among those who do, and
3. To consider the revenue from excise as secondary. Accordingly several measures are taken up by State Governments.

But these measures do not appear to have had any acceptable or salutary effect on Alcohol consumption. Subsequently, as a part of civil disobedience movement, Mahatma Gandhiji advocated the enforcement of complete prohibition of Alcohol. He wrote in "Young India" –

"If I was appointed as dictator for one hour for all India, the first thing I would do, would be to close without compensation, all liquor shops, destroy all toddy palms, compel factory owners to produce human conditions where these work men could get innocent drinks....". He even suggested to cut down the military expenditure to compensate the losses arise (Revenue from Excise) due to prohibition. But the outbreak of Second World War and the consequent situations in India lead to put a halt to the prohibition policy by Indian Governments. Hence, the implementation of the policy became ineffective and excise revenue started rising again. In fact, it was the single largest source of income for the government, by passing the land revenue. It is at this stage, first, the then : Madras state and then effectively, it is the Bombay state; have introduced prohibition in 1946-47. A separate law called the Bombay Prohibition Act, 1949 was brought towards complete prohibition with effect from April, 1950.

Beyond all, prohibition as an important state policy figures in the Directive Principles and according to Article 47 of the Indian Contribution.

"States shall endeavour to bring about prohibition of consumption, except for medical purpose, of intoxicating drinks and of drugs which are injurious to health."

As a sequel, the task of taking the responsibility of planning and implementation of the prohibition throughout the country was rested with the planning commission.

After a thorough enquiry by Srimannarayan Committee (1954-55), the Government has decided to bring about nation-wide prohibition by stages speedily and effectively. The Home Ministry set-up a central Prohibition Committee to examine the implementation of prohibition policy. Several measures such as, giving importance to voluntary and non-governmental organisations, providing financial assistance to all organisations to carry out social and educative programmes etc., were initiated.

In the year 1963, to review and suggest further towards the prohibition as a National Policy, the planning commission appointed a study team under the chairmanship of justice Tekchand. This report, which dealt with almost all aspects of liquour consumption in India.

After this, no significant efforts are made by the Government of India. People also did not talk much about this aspect. Further, the worsened economic conditions of India; have forced to keep the recommendations of justice Tekchand Committee cold storage. Almost all the states have liberalized the policies of prohibition and started concentrating on rising excise revenue.

Gandhian Ideology

Gandhiji's contribution to the problem of Alcohol consumption did not get as much attention as his struggle for freedom. But he has given utmost priority to make prohibition as a law, which ultimately resulted into the writings of India's first constitution of 1949. He said that alcoholism was one the major evils which needs to be eradicated in the country. He even advocated the consumption of 'Neera', the unfermented cell sap of the palms, as it would supply the necessary glucose and minerals to the body like coconut milk.

In 1925, Gandhiji argued that the most deplorable aspect, next to untouchability is the drink curse. Since the British rulers depended heavily on the revenues collected from the production and sale of alcohol, beverages, prohibition would revitalize our society and add strength to the struggle for national independence. He was so much against to the consumption of alcohol that he went to argue by saying " An alcohol addict is feeble -minded even when sober." According to him, the habit of drinking will follow insanity, adultery, gambling, and moral corruption etc., evils. He has stated that the cruel and crooked nature of Britishers was because of the habit of drinking alcohol; which depraves the mind and hardens the heart. Gandhi denied the argument that laws for bidding the sale of alcohol violated the drinker's rights. But he believed that they protect the would be drinker from himself.

Gandhiji, who is a lifelong teetotaler, had developed hostility towards consumption of alcohol, even before he became the leader of Indian national movement. He believed that teetotalism will lay foundation for healthful living, which can also be practiced by the poor. Some of his bitter experiences with Indian immigrant labour is South Africa and black Africans, are said to be the main reasons for converting Gandhiji to, complete prohibition. In his words, "I have seen with my own eyes the terrible scourge drink can be. It has ruined people morally, physically, economically and it has destroyed the sanctity and happiness of the home." In his book, key to Health, he reminded all, how drink had ruined the families of poor Indians. According to Gandhiji, poor Indian men wasted their major incomes on drink followed by street brawls, wife beating and child abuse.

Gandhiji's call for complete prohibition was initially subjected to criticism by some Marxists stating that it is all to distract the main issue of free India from others. But his approach has strengthened the movement with those people, by vision of a country free from the ill effects of alcohol consumption.

Gandhi's campaign for prohibition did not rest after it received a prominent plank in the Indian nationalist movement. Even after legislation, he encouraged peaceful picketing of Alcohol shops during his Satyagraha movement.

Gandhiji was equally continuous about the financial implications of prohibition. Once he has cheerfully suggested that the British could off set their losses by reducing military expenditure. Thus, he always used to dream of a dry India, free from the economic and social evils of Alcohol consumption and mainly a completely free India from Alcohol.

REFERENCES

1. O.M. Prakash: Food and Drinks in Ancient India.
2. Report of the Prohibition Enquiry Committee, 1954-55.
3. "Poverty and Purification: the Politics of Gandhiji Campaign for Prohibition" – Manian, Padma.
4. Internet.

24

Gandhian Thinking on Environment

P. Usha

Introduction

Environmental pollution is a grave concern today. The growing environmental challenge made Gandhian thinking a more relevant to the global crisis. Gandhi was well-known by all as a humanist, a political leader and pacifist of international fame. But a few know that he was an environmentalist too.

Environment provides us all amenity services not to pollute or destroy it. This obviously means that we have to enjoy environmental quality, without causing environmental pollution.

Environment acts as a supplier of resources and energy, on the one hand, and on the other hand, acts like a sink, to receive wastes from economic activities. If these wastes are biologically or chemically processed, then it will not draw the attention of environmentalists, but most of the wastes are not bio-degradable. These wastes will lie in the environment in its original form for years together. They create problems like genetic mutations, acid rain, and depletion of ozone layer, global warming and finally imbalance in the eco-system.

The unprecedented growth of population, increasing urbanization and rising standards of living have all leading to environmental stress through increase in both the amount and variety of waste generated. Some kinds of environmental degradation are truly global concern such as global warming and depletion of the ozone layer and others are localized like air pollution, water pollution, soil degradation, and desertification and so on.

Along with all these, waste disposal in urban areas is one of the major environmental problems. The "throw away societies" of cities generate the most trash disposal, which poses a major threat to environment.

Objectves

In this paper it is attempted to bring forth Gandhian thinking on environment and our endeavour here is to pin point the environment problems in slum areas. The main focus of the paper is to stress on the problems of waste disposal.

The problem of solid waste and waste water disposal can be checked with a little effort done by the people influencing Gandhian views on environment i.e. keep one's home and surroundings clean. If there is no environmental awareness among the people, in the future, more and more people will die of various diseases.

The 14th United Nations World Water Day report reveals the fact that, every 60 seconds, four children in the developing world die from water-related diseases mainly because of lack of safe drinking water and sanitation. With simple hygiene measures most of these deaths are preventable. Over 1 million people die from malaria every year. 1 billion people lack access to improved water supply. 2.4 billion People lack access to improved sanitation. In urban areas, more than 1 billion additional people will need access to both water supply and sanitation over next fifteen years in order to meet the targets.

In fact, the entire problem of environmental hazards, degradation is mainly because of industrialization and urbanization which adversely affects climatic conditions, to the awful disadvantages of living being, proliferation of slums. Gandhi is a profounder of a kind of life, culture and society which will never lead to environmental problems. The environmental friendly nature of Gandhian economic ideology is revealed when one notes the emphasis on the 'last-man'. In such policy, poverty has been described as the most severe polluter.

Growing urban population poses many problems like shortage of housing, safe drinking water, lack of drainage facilities, waste disposal etc. With increase in population and the rising demand for food and other essentials, there has been a rise in the amount of waste being generated daily by each household. And even the simple matter of waste disposal becomes problem.

In fact, slums are the origin of unsanitary conditions. The people live in slum areas live in unhygienic conditions. They do not have proper drainage facilities. The germs and other disease carrying vectors usually live in drainage water, which facilities their breeding and cause various diseases. Hence people should have awareness about their clean surroundings. Proper methods of waste disposal have to be undertaken to ensure that it does not effect the environment around the area or cause hazards to the people living there.

Gandhi believed that a good life can be lived in a small community. To him, big cities were centers of corruption and all kinds of vices. Therefore, he remained an ardent advocate of the village life throughout. He repeatedly said that India lived in her villages. What he tried to underline was that the soul of India lived there, that the village life is the ideal life and that India should live in villages. In fact, this is the universal prescription for a good life. It is a life of peace and tranquility, a life of innate simplicity and a life in a close proximity with nature. Such a life is also pone to the ethical.

Gandhi made honest efforts to translate his percepts in actual life. Throughout his life he kept on telling people and giving demonstration on health, hygiene and sanitation. Gandhi tried to carry the message to the mass through the life he himself led. He never employed sweeper in his house. Gandhi patterned his personal life and that of a small community on these ideas. He established ashrams on that pattern in South Africa and also in India. Gandhi persuaded the entire community of 125 boys and their teachers to run the kitchen, handle garbage, clean latrines, and sweep the grounds.[1]

Gandhi put emphasis on keeping one's home and surroundings clean. One of his test, in choose intimate in his ashram test, in choosing his inmate in ashram he cleaned his own toilet.[2]

In the age of growing urbanization, in spite of the sanitary facilities provided by the municipal authorities, the solid waste has been observed in many places. Of course, municipal authorities have arranged the dustbins, but neglects to collect the wastes from the bins and shift to the places of solid waste management. People are also careless about disposing of household garbage. They simply throw them near and there around the bins. But not keep them in proper places. Ultimately the waste spreads over the surroundings and animals and insects feed and disease carrying vectors breed there in. Huge domestic wastes being thoughtlessly dumped in drainage which comes in the way to flow drainage water into sewage management plant.

In this context, one should know the attitude of Gandhi towards the amenity services of environment. Everyday when Gandhi was taking bath in the freely flowing and unpolluted water of the sabarmati near ashram.

Consciously used only the minimum requisite water needed for taking bath. On being asked why he was using the river water so sparingly when it was available in abundance, he remarked that all that was flowing in the river was not his. Of course here he talked about the minimum consumption of natural resources like water the most important natural resource without which we cannot live. But now-a-days people are not even hesitate to pollute water which becomes scarce at present.

Suggestions

Now the question is how to stop all this thoughtless activities of waste disposal.

1. In order to overcome the problem, proper methods of waste disposal have to be undertaken to ensure that it does not affect the environment or cause health hazards to the people. If cleanliness is maintained then pollution in one way can be checked. If people keep themselves clean along with the environment, it would be a good thing for man kind. People should not think that only the government is responsible for maintaining cleanliness. But each individual should co-operate and keeps the environment clean.
2. Many environmentalists suggest that people's participation in keeping environment clean is the only way to over come the problem of waste disposal. The time has come to spread out Gandhian views on environment by impressing the people to do their job in order to promote community solidarity in making them self-reliant in keeping

environment clean, without depending on municipal authorities.

Thus, I end by saying that creating environmental awareness is important especially, among slum dwellers, to reduce the problems of waste disposal on the Gandhian lines i.e., keep one's home and surroundings clean.

REFERENCES

1. The Life of Mahatma Gandhi by Louis Fischer.
2. Gandhi by M.K. Mahajan.

25

Enduring Significance of the Dandi March

S.N. Sahu

Dandi March was an unprecedented and unique event not only in the history of India but also in the history of mankind surpassing the importance, method scope and objective of possibly any other movement and march, started at any time and anywhere in the world for freedom and independence. It is well-known that it revolved around the breaking of the salt law, which triggered the civil disobedience movement and aimed' at achieving independence for our country. Entirely planned, designed and executed by Mahatma Gandhi, it was an epoch making March which lasted only for 26 days electrified the nation, awakened the world with its moral momentum and spiritual appeal and shook the very foundation of the British Empire. Beginning on, March 12 it concluded on April 6, 1930 and encompassed in its scope the goal of political and economic independence and all-round progress, of what Mahatma Gandhi caned, the dumb millions of our country.

It was a historic March undertaken by him following the resolution he moved in the Lahore session of the Indian National Congress in December 1929 demanding complete independence for our country. It has to be studied and analysed to understand its deep significance not only for the cause of our independence and our country but also for the cause of the world and the whole of humanity in the context of the problems and challenges of our age. It is eternally relevant for the issues it raised and the method it adopted arid the manner in which it involved the vast masses of ordinary women and men in its marvellous and morally uplifting battle of right against might.

One, of the fascinating and absorbing aspects of the Dandi March was the way Gandhiji reached out to the people from all sections of society, particularly the ordinary men and women and the underprivileged and downtrodden among them, and sought their support for the great March. His personal life of extraordinary simplicity and his identification with the common people of our country inspired and motivated them to follow him. But the way he appealed to their intellect and heart by understanding their suffering and exploitation and explaining to their suffering and exploitation and explaining to them about the reality in an intelligible manner helped them to comprehend their objective social and economic conditions and the need to change those by participating in the struggle for independençe. For example, he did not straightaway take up the high minded ideals of liberty and equality and tell them that the British rulers denied these to them and therefore they should rise against the foreign rule and oppression. He made them understand about these ideals by educating them about the disparity of daily income between an average Indian and the then Viceroy of India and compared it with the average daily income of an average Briton with the daily income of the them British Prime Minister. He pointed out that while the daily income of an average Indian was only 12 paise, the British Viceroy's daily salary was Rs. 700. He brought to the knowledge of the common people that wile the British Viceroy was getting much over five thousand time India's average income, the British rime Minister was getting only ninety times Britain's average income. On March 2, 1930, that is 10 days before he commenced the famous Dandi March he wrote to the then Viceroy of India Lord Irwin about these chilling figures, conveyed him the crushing burden of the Zamindari system and exorbitant land revenue on the ordinary peasants and cultivators and thoroughly outlined the exploitation suffered by the people of India and the moral and spiritual degradation they were subjected to under the colonial rule.

Giving reasons as to why he regarded the British rule a curse, he explained in that incisive letter to the Viceroy:

> It has impoverished the dumb millions by a system of progressive exploitation and by a ruinously expensive military and civil administration which the country can never afford.

Stating that people were desperate and restless to liberate themselves from such an exploitative system he told the Viceroy the meaning of independence as understood by ordinary people. He wrote: "To them independence means deliverance from the killing weight." Gandhiji thus interpreted independence in terms of the needs and aspirations of the common people and informed them and communicated with them in that language only. With rare sensitivity he understood the pulse and hearts and minds of the people.

He felt that by choosing the issue which would be common to all and because of which the poverty stricken people of Indian are suffering the most and which can unite the people inhabiting the length and breadth of the country he could make ordinary people the main force behind independence and its principal beneficiaries. He informed the Viceroy that independence was essentially for the poorest in the land and he would strive for it through the Civil Disobedience Movement by violating the provisions of the salt law as he regarded the tax on salt "to be the most iniquitous of all from the poor man's stand point." Gandhiji communicated these facts to the people, informed them about their social and economic conditions and made them aware of their duty to join the struggle for independence.

During the March he, through his speeches and writings, was driving home these points form enlisting their support. It constituted a remarkable effort to inform people who had the right to know about the cause of their suffering. Each step Gandhiji was taking during the March was a giant step for the right to information. In a way he was spearheading a revolutionary movement for the right to information which is now at the heart of the movement launched by the people for empowering themselves with information and which is considered central to deepen democracy and good governance.

One of the enduring lessons of the Dandi March was the right of the people over the natural resources which legitimately belonged to them. Gandhiji by choosing salt as the main theme of the civil disobedience movement was challenging the monopoly of natural resources by the mighty and the powerful. The central message of a Dandi March was in fact the equitable distribution of resources so that the dumb millions to whom such resources legitimately belonged could become their owners. In the letter he wrote to Viceroy Lord Irwin on March 2, 1930, which has been referred to earlier, Gandhiji wondered as to how" we have submitted to the cruel monopoly for so long." In fact on April 10, 1930, four days after the completion of the March, in an article in Young India he wrote:

> The British Empire was conceived in immorality, for it was to perpetuate the exploitation of India's resources that it was founded.

The Dandi March, by harnessing the power of the ordinary people, aimed at restoring the right of the people on the resource of the nation. The day when ordinary people are in the forefront of the struggle for environmental protection and sustainable development, the message of the Dandi March for fighting against the reckless exploitation of natural resources assume enormous significance.

One of the disturbing and dangerous trends of our time is the upsurge of forces which harp on exclusiveness and foster a conter culture which as dealt a heavy blow on the inclusive society, identity and outlook of our country. To fight against such forces and to defeat them we need to drive appropriate lessons from the Dandi March. The entire plan of Mahatma Gandhi to undertake the March was based on an inclusive approach. He wrote the letter to the Viceroy, which was a blue-print for our freedom from British rule and exploitation and asked a British gentleman, Mr. Reynolds, to carry it to the Viceroy. By selecting a British national to hand over the letter to the British Government he was consciously sending a powerful message to the rest of the world—that our struggle for swarag was based on the support of all section of society including the English people. He wrote:

> It was neither empty formulation nor a touch of vanity that prompted me to send a English friend with my letter to the Viceroy. By choosing Reginald Reynolds as my messenger, I sealed the bond between them and me. For my enmity is not against them, it is against their rule.

The universal vision behind the Dandi March needs to be invoked to strengthen our inclusive society.

In the same letter he accused the British Government of all the time invoking the communal problem plaguing the land and sidestepping the real exploitation of people to perpetuate the colonial rule. He wrote:

> You have unnecessarily laid stress upon the communal problem that unhappily affect this land. Important though they undoubtedly are for the consideration of any scheme of government, they have little bearing on the greater problems which are above communities and which affect them all equally.

In fact by taking up the issue of salt he transcended the narrow confines of communal and caste barriers and brought about the unity of people professing diverse faiths. The way he opposed the salt tax was not only novel but also revealing for our times. He referred to the scriptures of all religions, drew from them support and strength to advance his argument that the poor and women should be exempted from tax and sensitized people that the British law imposing a heavy tax on salt was against the injunctions all religious tenets and caused untold suffering on the poor and the downtrodden of all communities. Thus combining the religious and rational approach to explain the phenomenon of economic exploitation under British rule he appealed to the heads and hearts of all communities, enlisted the support of members of all denominations and prepared a common front against British rule for achieving independence in a non-violent manner.

Two days before Gandhiji started the Dandi March Shaukat Ali, who joined hands with him during the Khilafat movement and eloquently proclaimed Hindu-Muslim unity, accused Gandhiji that his March would herald a Hindu Raj in India. Gandhiji not only refuted the accusation but declared on the day of commencement of the March, that is on March 12, 1930 that he along with his fellow workers were the trustees of Hindu-Muslim unity. While marching towards Dandi a young man from the Muslim community asked him a question regarding the future legislature of India and wanted to know the number of seats the Muslim community would get for their representatives. In his own characteristic way he replied:

> Give me a seat in the legislative assembly only if there is any left after giving them to Muslims, Parsis, Christians and all others.

The breadth of his vision, his broadminded approach and his tolerant outlook remained the driving force behind the Dandi March and need to be invoked to counter the divisive tendencies which today stoke the flames of communalism and put at stake our unity, composite cultural ethos and above all invite international opprobrium for themselves and for the country.

As the March was proceeding from Sabarmati to Dandi large numbers of Muslims, Christains and members of all other religious groupings lined the route, extended moral and material support to Gandhi and his fellow-marchers and blessed them to be successful in their mission. He received wide support from all communities for the cause of breaking the salf law. To dispel any notion that Muslims are aggrieved with him, he accepted the invitation from a Muslim friend from Dandi to stay in his house and declared that he would commence the Satyagraph from there. This message of unity among all religious communities is of paramount importance in the context of what happened in Gujarat between February and May 2002 and which has caused pain and suffering to all communities while tarnishing the image of India in the comity of nations.

It is well-known that Gandhiji was a deeply religious person, had a profound spiritual outlook and was a critique of organized religion. When he undertook the Dandi March he was sixty-one years of age. Many suggested to him that the real *dharma* for a man of his age was to go the Himalayas for the purpose of seeing God and attaining the liberation of soul. But his reply that he had learnt an opposite *dharma* and wanted to have a *darshan* of God through the March and by identifying himself with thirty crores of people of India, constituted a refreshing approach to religion which stands far above superstition, rituals and orthodoxy and upholds humanism and service to the humanity. He redefined theism and said a beliver in God was one who established at heart unity with Muslims, Sikhs, Parsis, Christians, Sikhs and men and women of every section of each community. In our own time when a counter culture of superstition and outmoded practices has been able to distort religious beliefs and practices and blinds the people's perceptions while prompting them to take resort to violent and inhuman actions, it is pertinent to hark back to Mahatma Gandhi who redefined *dharma* as service of the people and who described the Dandi March as a sacred pilgrimage in quest of spirituality and purification of mind an body. Religion ceases to be religion if it is used to promote hatred and animosity and divide people and cause bloodshed among them.

One of the striking features of the Dandi March was the enthusiastic role played by women in supporting the March and actively participating in it. As part of the larger plan for the Civil Disobedience Movement they also carried out other activities such as promotion of Khadi, picketing of liquor shops and cleaning of villages and making rural people aware of the values and importance of sanitation and hygiene for keeping themselves healthy and free from disease. During the Dandi March Mahatma Gandhi appealed for support from all sections of society. Women responded to Gandhiji's call, came out in large numbers leaving their homes and families and involved themselves in doing everything possible to make it successful. They displayed remarkable courage and heroism in coming out of the four walls of the home and taking part in one of the greatest struggles of making for freedom and independence. Mahatma Gandhi himself acknowledged:

> ...in this struggle for freedom, the contribution of women will exceed that of men.

He lamented that the burden of domestic work kept women away from the public life and deprived the nation of their service. In fact during the March when Gandhiji asked the village women if they knew Jawaharlal Nehru they said, "How can we know?" Stating that he women were not at fault for the ignorance, he blamed the attitude and otlook which was responsible for keeping them as house-keepers, cooks, scavengers and drawers of water. He was hopeful that with the success of the March and the Civil Disobedience Movement the share of women in every activity of life would as big as that of men.

Women did come out of the narrow domestic walls and played a key role in galvanizing the Civil Disobedience Movement and becoming its torchbearers. The upsurge of women marked a new era for their awakening and empowerment. The publication of the British Government entitled "India in 1930-31" wrote:

> Thousands of them – many being of good family and high educational attainments-suddenly emerged from the seclusion of their homes, and in some instance actually from

> purdah, in order to join the Congress demonstrations and assist in picketing, and their presence on these occasions made the work the police were required to perform particularly unpleasant.

The progress of women in India owes a lot to the Dandi March started by Gandhiji 75 years ago and this needs to be carried forward with redoubled vigour so that they, in the words of Mahatma, have as big as men's share in national affairs.

The Dandi March was a march for the health of our people and nation. The lesson of the Dandi March for building the health of our people assumes enormous significance. One may be a little curious to find out as to how a March conceived to break the salt law and start the Civil Disobedience Movement could have any link with the health of our people. In fact, during the March some of the marchers suffered from fever, some had swelling on their feet and one of them suffered from mild small pox. Mahatma Gandhi described them as small accidents and said that a lesson should be drawn from them. He wondered how his fellow marchers could not withstand the strain of twenty kilometers of walk daily and had to suffer fatigue and tiredness. Even though he was a sixty-one-year-old man and was walking faster than others nothing happened to him. He was distressed by the lack of strength of those who walked with him and wrote on April 3, 1930, three days before he broke the salt law, about the need to do exercises.

> The modern generation is delicate, weak, and much pampered. If they will take part in national work they must take ample exercise and become hardy. And no exercise is as good as and as effective as long vigorous marches. Gymnastics and the like are good and many be added to walking. They are no substitutes for walking, justly called the prince of exercises.

The modern generation he referred to has become weaker, extremely, delicate and remained vulnerable to cardiovascular diseases, hypertension and diabetes due to reduced physical activity and therefore the prescription of Mahatma Gandhi for ample exercises through long and fast walk and gymnastics is relevance for all time to come.

In fact, a deeper analysis of his remarkable insights for keeping ourselves physically fit. Before he started the March he wrote a detailed note outlining the way food would be prepared for the consumption of those who were participating in the March. He strictly prohibited the use of oil and spices to keep the health of the volunteers fit for the 240 kilometre walk. During the March when some enthusiastic workers used vehicles to get milk from Surat he felt sad and remarked, "Do not resort to motor cars on the slightest pretext. The rule is, do not ride if you can walk." The proliferation of motorized transport and the increase of cars and vehicles per family and person have caused many health problems in developed courtiers. The same trend is emerging in our country and people are using the cars and other motor transport in the slightest pretext. "The rule." As Gandhiji said, "do not ride if you can walk." This is a catchy health slogan coined during the Dandi March by the Father of our Nation almost in anticipation of the terrific increase of vehicle population and our use of such modes of transport at the grave risk of our health, money and fuel. This too constitutes the enduring relevance of the Dandi March for our critical times.

Index